Can Science Resolve the Nature/Nurture Debate?

New Human Frontiers series

Can Science Resolve the Nature/Nurture Debate?

MARGARET LOCK &
GISLI PALSSON

polity

First published in 2016 by Polity Press

Polity Press
65 Bridge Street
Cambridge CB2 1UR, UK

Polity Press
350 Main Street
Malden, MA 02148, USA

ISBN-13: 978-0-7456-8996-8
ISBN-13: 978-0-7456-8997-5 (pb)

A catalogue record for this book is available from the British Library.

Library of Congress Cataloging-in-Publication Data

Names: Lock, Margaret. | Gisli Palsson, 1949-
Title: Can science resolve the nature-nurture debate? / Margaret Lock, Gisli Palsson.
Description: Cambridge, UK : Polity, 2016. | Includes bibliographical references and index.
Identifiers: LCCN 2015044017 (print) | LCCN 2015049073 (ebook) | ISBN 9780745689968 (hardback) | ISBN 9780745689975 (pbk.) | ISBN 9780745689999 (Mobi) | ISBN 9780745690001 (Epub)
Subjects: LCSH: Nature and nurture. | Human genetics. | Genetics. | Human biology.
Classification: LCC QH438.5 .L63 2016 (print) | LCC QH438.5 (ebook) | DDC 616/.042—dc23
LC record available at http://lccn.loc.gov/2015044017

Typeset in 11 on 15 pt Adobe Garamond Pro Regular
by Toppan Best-set Premedia Limited
Printed and bound in United Kingdom by Clays Ltd, St Ives PLC

For further information on Polity, visit our website:
politybooks.com

Nature is perhaps the most complex word in the language.
Raymond Williams, *Keywords*, 1976

We must seek to understand the emergent and irreducible property arising from an inextricable interpenetration of genes and environment.
Stephen Jay Gould, *An Urchin in the Storm*, 1987

CONTENTS

The following people have generously taken time to share their expertise with us, which, on occasion, was urgently needed: Evelyn Fox Keller, Hannah Landecker, Richard Lock, Margaret McFall-Ngai, Jörg Niewöhner, Barbara Prainsack, and Faith Wallis. We are also indebted to two anonymous reviewers for their insightful and encouraging comments. Finally, we would like to thank everyone at Polity Press, who have been exceptionally supportive throughout the preparation of this book.

Beyond the Molecular Vision of Life

Numerous people take it for granted today that genes cause certain kinds of developmental problems and diseases. Down syndrome comes to mind, as do images of Stephen Hawking wheelchair-bound with motor neuron disease. But these same people assume that, in addition to genes, lifestyle and environment are implicated to varying degrees in conditions such as heart and lung diseases, asthma, obesity, and diabetes. In other words, poor habits and toxic environments somehow interact with genes, with negative consequences. Researchers are likely to express this situation in terms of the percentage input from genes and environment respectively involved in any given condition. Conversely, "healthy" lifestyles and environments can be protective.

The burgeoning field of epigenetics challenges received wisdom about the relationship – and relative importance – of genes and environment, nature and nurture. From the early twentieth century, following recognition of the significance of Gregor Mendel's work on pea plants, an assumption gradually took hold among numerous geneticists that genes fully account for human biology and behavior. This position was consistently countered for the next few decades by researchers who argued that human behavioral traits develop almost exclusively from environmental influences, following John Locke's late seventeenth-century idea of a *tabula rasa*. However, the demonstration of the existence of DNA and its helical structure in the 1950s ensured that genetic determinism under the designation of "The New Synthesis" was rapidly consolidated as the dominant approach to understanding life itself.

Massive infusions of money were put into research in genetics, and critics of gene-centrism, biologists and social scientists alike, of whom there were a good number, were largely ignored. Now epigeneticists have added a strong voice to this critique, one grounded in molecular biology, and the century-long assumption, held by numerous scientists, that genes are the controlling force of life has been badly shaken by these claims to the contrary.

Epigenetics literally means "over or above genetics," but its concise meaning changes and becomes further elaborated as new discoveries come to light. A few years ago, scientists in the expanding subfield of behavioral epigenetics claimed that they had uncovered molecular links *between* nature and nurture, that is, evidence that nature/nurture is not divisible. This assertion was based on research demonstrating how environmental stimuli and stressors originating externally and internally to the body initiate trains of molecular activity that modifies how DNA functions during individual development, at times with life-long effects on human behavior and wellbeing. The epigenetic mechanism best researched to date is methylation, a process initiated by enzymes in which DNA *sequences* are not changed, but one nucleotide, cytosine, is converted to 5-methylcytocine, resulting in changes to the shape or character of the nucleotide base, thus rendering a portion of DNA inactive. Protein methylation also takes place. Animal research has shown that methylation modifications can even be transmitted intergenerationally.

Debates about the locus of responsibility for malaise and disease, policy making relating to human wellbeing, and discussion about social justice in connection with healthcare are increasingly taking epigenetic findings into consideration, a move that will have wide-ranging social and political consequences.

The ubiquity of hype

In the first years of the twenty-first century, when mapping the human genome was close to completion, many experts and members of the public alike thought that with the "blueprint of life" in our hands, substantial improvements in health, illness, and wellbeing would soon follow. The hyperbole before and during the tedious process of mapping the genome was extraordinary. As early as 1988, the United States Office of Technology Assessment claimed that emerging genetic information would bring about a "eugenics of normalcy," ensuring that "each individual has at least a modicum of normal genes." It was claimed that eugenic practices carried out since the early part of the twentieth century would from now on be achieved through "technological" as opposed to "social controls," thus achieving "a paramount right to be born with a normal, adequate, hereditary endowment" (United States Office of Technology Assessment 1988: 86).

A second report, *Predictive Medicine*, published in 1988 by the European Commission, claimed that individuals would be protected from the kinds of illnesses to which they are most vulnerable, and transmission of genetic susceptibilities to the next generation would be prevented. This "neo-eugenics," as it was termed, designed to detect and abort "unsuitable" fetuses through the implementation of genetic screening programs, was fostered in the 1980s and early 1990s with the blessing of Margaret Thatcher and like-minded

European politicians, specifically in order to reduce future healthcare expenditure. Extensive critical commentary by German Greens, activist Catholics, and certain conservative politicians, however, ensured that "predictive medicine" was never funded.

Following completion of the Human Genome Project, another round of promises were made, among them the development of personalized drugs, and the prevention of common diseases through the detection and modification of genes. These endeavours have had limited success, although significant advances in genotyping cancer tumors have improved treatment outcomes and a powerful new technology that enables editing of specific genes has enormous potential.

Epigenetic findings have raised the stakes enormously – some claim that a paradigm shift is taking place, and a new round of hype has appeared. On the cover of its issue for January 6, 2010, *Time* magazine displayed the unzipping of the DNA double helix under the title "Why your DNA isn't your destiny: The new science of epigenetics reveals how the choices you make can change your genes – and those of your kids." The related article by John Cloud suggests that a single winter of overeating as a youngster can initiate a biological chain of events eventually contributing to the death of one's grandchildren.

The number of publications carrying "epigenetics" in their titles in 2010 amounted to a stunning 20,000. Since then, success stories have rapidly escalated. The annual number of papers with either "epigenetics" or "epigenetic" in their titles indexed by WorldCat from 2011 to 2015 is 25,208 (books, theses, journal articles, and book chapters). In comparison, annual figures prior to 1995 were in two digits or less. Googling the word "epigenetics" in late 2015 yielded 3.5 million hits, and a molecular biologist claims that this new discipline is "revolutionising biology" (Carey 2012: 6). Research is underway to develop pharmaceutical interventions to reverse epigenetic changes, although this is virtually confined thus far to the management of cancer. A significant transformation is apparently brewing in the world of molecular biology, and while some dismiss this as a transient bubble, they are doing so with less and less conviction as time passes.

Bridging two cultures

In 1959, the chemist and novelist C.P. Snow published the now classic book *Two Cultures*, in which he lamented that intellectual life in "western society" was divided between the sciences and the humanities – a split, he argued, that hindered efforts to solve the world's problems. Such a division is strikingly evident today within the academic field of anthropology (our own speciality): research into human "nature" – biological evolution and variation – has been divorced from research into "nurture" – the social, economic, political, and cultural contexts in which people live.

A 2012 editorial in *Nature* (490, 11) suggests that, in light of recent developments in epigenetics and related fields, the time is overdue for social scientists and biologists "to bury the hatchet" and abandon the long-standing "fortresses" of nature and nurture. But it is one thing to transcend the hostile intellectual domains of previous generations, and quite another to form a united effort to address the growing recognition among many researchers in the biological and social sciences respectively of the entanglement of biology in environmental, social, and political relations. To date, there are few signs of a fundamental change in orientation. On the contrary, it is evident that the molecular endpoints of epigenetic activity detected inside the body are capturing most attention in both the research world and the media, thus setting to one side the numerous factors external to the body that contribute to distress and disease throughout life.

Epigeneticists often "miniaturize" nurture in order to standardize their research practices. For example, it has been shown that exposure of a fetus *in utero* to maternal stress and anxiety can have post-natal effects that may last for years, possibly a lifetime. Researchers attribute this to "epigenetic dysregulation" that occurred during pregnancy. The reality of the everyday lives of so many pregnant women – such as lack of money to buy food and clothing and inadequate housing – is sidelined by the majority of investigators in their search for measurable evidence of the embodiment of trauma, stress, and noxious chemicals.

Such evidence is important, but the *origins* of many epigenetic marks present in individual bodies can only be comprehensively accounted for by attending to history, politics, and social relations. Human bodies are not skin-bound, and the domains of the social and biological are inseparably coalesced from the moment of conception. Attempting to depict the impact of unrelenting exposure to poverty, violence, discrimination, and racism on individuals, families, and groups of people demands more than bodily evidence to give a satisfactory account of what has taken place. A chronicle of the lives of present and previous generations as recalled by living family members is important, because epigenetic marks reveal abuse endured not solely in the present but also in the past. Whether or not epigenetic changes are transmitted intergenerationally in humans remains a matter for heated debate, but if this proves not to be the case, irrefutable evidence shows that epigenetic changes arise anew in ensuing generations if living conditions are not substantially improved.

Not only do environmental stimuli, external and internal to the body, impinge on an embryo from the moment of inception, but the embryo is always already a creature of the past – it has a history: the lasting effects of evolutionary, environmental, historical, cultural, and stochastic (unpredictable) variables, to which the DNA of previous generations have continually been exposed over eons of time. When reproduction takes place, the haploid form (half the chromosomes) of the genomes of the egg and sperm contribute their histories – their cell memories – to the conceptus. Thus, certain of the embodied effects of the lived experiences of one's parents and of earlier ancestors are transferred to ensuing generations. No systematic causal trails link nurture writ large, that is, environments past and present, with individual genotypes – such pathways are neither linear nor inevitable – but, as the biologist Steven Rose puts it, this "alternative vision of living systems… recaptures an understanding of living organisms and their trajectories through time and space as lying at the centre of biology" (1997: 7).

Along similar lines, the anthropologist Tim Ingold insists that "process" should take priority over "form" and that humans, and indeed creatures of all kinds, should be recognized "not as *beings* but as *becomings*...who continually forge their ways, and guide the ways of consociates, in the crucible of their common life. In so doing, they weave a kind of tapestry. But like life itself, the tapestry is never complete, never finished. It is always a work in progress" (Ingold 2013: 8). A commingling of nature/nurture exists from conception, to which deep history contributes. The molecular aspects of this ceaseless work in progress take two forms: first, ordered, epigenetically controlled bodily development, without which none of us would live; and, second, the action of environmental variables on the genome throughout life, affecting gene expression, with both positive and negative outcomes. Inevitably, dysregulation occurs – a sign of the wear and tear of life itself and, in later life, of aging. In situations of impoverishment, dysregulation can accumulate relentlessly from gestation on, resulting in great rents in the tapestry.

The position we take is that science cannot resolve nature/nurture debates. In effect, such debates are a red herring because nature and nurture are not readily demarcated objects of scientific inquiry. On the contrary, these concepts have been movable targets throughout history, the result of endless tussles about their relationship to one another, and the delineation of their boundaries. Throughout the twentieth century, the dominant understanding was that nature and nurture were clearly divisible entities. But insights accrued from epigenetics from the latter part of the twentieth century, rapidly accumulating each year, are bringing about an ontological shift, in which nature and nurture are understood by epigeneticists, developmental biologists, embryologists, certain philosophers of biology, and an array of social scientists as always already mingled from the moment of conception; thus, boundaries formerly assumed to be clearly demarcated are dissolved, with repercussions for medical, political, and family accounts about responsibility for ill health.

Epigenetics is a young science, and not well accepted by researchers wedded to a reductionistic way of thought. Several leading researchers in epidemiology and the biological sciences argue forcefully for recognition of unpredictable events that limit the very possibility of documenting straightforward cause-and-event pathways from environments, external and internal to the body, to detectable molecular marks of embodied stress. The unknowns are numerous, among them why epigenetic marks often reverse quite quickly, and why many people who have undergone severe trauma prove to be resilient against all odds.

Moreover, epigenetic arguments are evolving, and innovative questions and new technologies will keep the kaleidoscope turning continually, transforming discussion about the relationship of nature/nurture. No doubt, at times, laboratory-based epigeneticists will declare that they have solved the puzzle once and for all. Meanwhile, the social and political origins of ill health and traumatized lives will remain unaccounted for, no matter how scientifically accurate is the documentation of embodied epigenetic marks.

Our position is that socioeconomic and political contributions to bodily distress must be taken very seriously. If not, epigenetics may become mired in a form of neo-reductionism that, even though it facilitates drug development to reverse epigenetic marks, is not sufficient. A science of epigenetically induced pathology, resembling the dominant approach in biomedicine, will not facilitate a paradigm shift; if accounts of causality originating in the environment writ large are left unattended to, or situated entirely within families, then the political significance of epigenetic findings will be impoverished. In the latter half of this book, we suggest how such an endpoint might be avoided. These ideas will not foreclose nature/nurture debates, but may nudge them in what we regard as a positive direction.

ONE

Movable Concepts: Nature and Nurture

In contemporary European languages, the word "nature" is derived from a Latin translation of the Greek *physis*. Etymologically, the meaning stems from both *natura* ("the course of things") and *nascere* ("to be born"). Raymond Williams, claiming that nature is "perhaps the most complex word in the language" (1976: 219), noted that when it refers to the material world itself, humans can be either included or excluded as part of nature. Furthermore, nature refers to the idea of an inherent force that directs either the world, or human beings, or both, giving nature a moral authority. In addition, "natural" implies the essential quality or character of something, and with respect to humans it is frequently used to convey that which is given from birth. Intellectual debates over the centuries have set nature in opposition to history, art, law, civilization, society, and nurture, among other ideas and institutions.

In this book, we will be concerned with the concepts "nature" and "nurture" and how and why their relationship one with the other mutates over time and across space. Our account dwells primarily on significant changes over the past two centuries in Europe, but this first chapter sets out the longer history of human understandings of the causes of health and disease, beginning in classical Greece, where philosophers, dramatists, poets, and physicians, together with countless others, participated in debates about conception, the unfolding of life in the womb, and the relationship of environments and behaviors to health and disease. Such debates persisted through the centuries, modified by empirical findings and new insights, and it was not until the mid-nineteenth century that the situation changed dramatically in Europe. Francis Galton, a polymath if ever there was one (anthropologist, tropical explorer, geographer, inventor of fingerprint identification, meteorologist, psychometrician, geneticist, and statistician), is usually credited with coining the phrase "nature and nurture" and set out his position in 1874:

[Nature and nurture] is a convenient jingle of words, for it separates under two distinct heads the innumerable elements of which personality is composed. Nature is all that a man brings with himself into the world; nurture is every influence from without that affects him after birth. The distinction is clear: the one produces the infant such as it actually is; including its latent faculties of growth of body and mind; the other affords the environment amid which the growth takes place, by which natural tendencies may be strengthened or thwarted, or wholly new ones implanted. (Galton 1874: 12)

Galton insisted that nature and nurture be researched as separable, objective entities. He regarded nature as the origin of life itself, affected by nurture only after birth, and not *in utero*. He also challenged an assumption about the inheritance of acquired characteristics present in Europe from antiquity to the mid-eighteenth century.

Nature and nurture in classical Europe

The Hippocratic School is credited with breaking away from beliefs about disease causation that were dominant in the fifth century BCE. Philosophers and medical practitioners alike created a language that left no room for divine intervention or caprice, and the idea was gradually accepted of "regularities" in the natural world that even the gods could not violate. The term *physis*, often translated as "nature," was used to indicate inevitable variation that could be understood by reason. A second term, *technê* ("art"), was adopted to describe professional expertise and practice based on knowledge of these natural regularities. These terms were already present in the Greek language before Hippocrates' time, and may have had Mesopotamian and Egyptian origins, but the Hippocratic School deliberately transformed their meanings.

Despite its recognition of natural clustered regularities, the Hippocratic corpus makes clear that many different natures exist, and these are not unified as one. Human beings have a shared *physis*, but each individual also has a singular *physis*. Furthermore, *physis* varies according to gender, age, and individual strength or weakness. Food and drink have their own *physis*, as do the ingredients of medication. Inevitably, disagreements existed among practitioners, but Hippocrates wrote that the key entities – air, water, places – each have a distinct *physis*.

By conceptualizing humans as embedded in their respective geographical and climatic environments, Hippocrates sought to create a unifying theory of health and illness. The notion of a harmonious balance sustained through moderation was dominant, and the task of physicians was to detect imbalances and restore fundamental order to the bodies of patients. Key to health and disease was an understanding of how the humors – phlegm, blood, yellow bile, and black bile – change according to the seasons, and also according to local factors such as the quality of the wind and water and the orientation of towns and villages. Individual "character" was also significant, and moderation was encouraged with respect to diet, behavior, and climatic exposure.

Aristotle wrote extensively about disease causation, and a flood of commentary ensued based on his canon, produced in the third century BCE; these exchanges, often very argumentative, persisted throughout the medieval period. Aristotle followed Hippocrates in recognizing humors, and subsumed them with other entities into a category labeled "naturals," understood as intrinsic to the body. Naturals could not be voluntarily controlled. A second group of entities, extrinsic to the body, was subdivided into "non-naturals" and "contra-naturals." Counter-intuitively to us moderns, non-naturals included such items as food and drink, exercise and rest, sleep and wakefulness, repletion and evacuation, and the emotions, over all of which necessities and states humans were expected to maintain a degree of control. Entities recognized as diseases were labeled as contra-naturals.

It is striking that whenever physicians who followed Aristotelian thinking detected an entity believed to stabilize the state of the body, it was regarded as "intrinsic," whether located inside or outside the physical body. Conversely, any agent regarded as bringing about destabilization was declared to be "extrinsic," whether or not it was located inside the body. Humors, for example, were recognized as intrinsic to the body, but could become extrinsic when they brought about an imbalance. Alien, disruptive forces could exist inside the body, but, for the most part, such disruptive events originated from activities and events outside the body. Non-natural emotions were particularly prone to traversing the extrinsic/intrinsic boundary – the human body was porous.

According to Aristotle, "soul" (*psyche*) constitutes the form or essence of any living thing and is fundamental to bodily activities of all kinds, ranging from movement to thought. Distributed throughout the body, "soul" cannot exist independently, nor is it associated especially with mental activities. Certain commentators have suggested that the Aristotelian "soul" is best understood as equivalent to "lifeforce," and Aristotle is credited with encouraging practitioners of Hellenistic medicine to develop knowledge about health in addition to disease.

The physician Galen, born in Pergamum in the first century CE, made no effort to define soul, stating that one could never develop logical proof of its existence. He declared that he had no interest in metaphysics, was opposed to speculation, and practiced animal dissection and vivisection in order to understand anatomy and physiology. However, Galen retained the early Greek idea of *pneuma*, or "breath," as the fundamental animating force within the body, and made it central in his elaboration of humoral medicine, in which the body is conceptualized as a microcosm of the all-encompassing spheres of the macrocosm. This theory, in which balance was the key concept, was debated and elaborated while Galen was alive and persisted long after his death. Followers of Galen disseminated humoral medicine worldwide as they traveled throughout the Middle East, North Africa, and Europe, and later colonizers carried it further afield to the Americas and the Philippines. With its focus on interactions between bodies and environments, it remained the most widely used form of medical knowledge until well into the nineteenth century.

The tenacity of humoral medicine

Medical anthropologists have documented how, in the geographical locations where humoral medicine was adopted and is often still practiced, it infuses everyday knowledge about health and illness. Close attention is paid to the oppositional forces of "hot" and "cold" and "wet" and "dry" in daily life, entities with both literal and metaphorical connotations. Illnesses such as a cold, asthma, and other bronchial problems are associated with heat – with "fever," including what today would be diagnosed as malaria. And pregnancy, too, contributes to a build-up of heat. Humoral theory places moderation in behavior and daily life at the core of its moral discourse; individuals are expected to follow a regimen that maintains an appropriate balance, and only thus can danger be averted.

The four classical literate medical traditions (which emerged independently of each other) are grounded in microcosm/macrocosm homologies. Unani-Tibb evolved directly from Galenism to become formalized throughout the Islamic world and much of Eastern Europe as the dominant medical system. The Ayurvedic tradition, which had its origins in the Vedas, took firm hold in India, and the indigenous Chinese medical system, the oldest written medical tradition, eventually spread to

Japan in the sixth century CE. Significant historical differences exist among these traditions, and theorizing and practice have been modified over time, but balance and harmony are key concepts in all, as is the idea of "breath" or "*chi*" being fundamental to life. Bodies are understood as inextricably embedded in environments, with the result that no distinction was made between nature and nurture.

These literate traditions continue to flourish, and Chinese medicine and Ayurveda both have a global reach. The primary objective of patient care remains that of restoration of balance to the body, even though extensive knowledge and training in contemporary biomedicine is common among many practitioners. In Japan, for example, all practitioners of acupuncture, and many of those who work as masseuses, are fully trained in anatomy and physiology. In order to be licensed, practitioners of herbal medicine must be in possession of an MD in addition to years of formal training in their own specialty. These physicians choose between two standardized ways of going about diagnosis – and treatment – depending upon the presentation of symptoms by patients. At the first visit, extensive histories are taken in order to establish how the environment and everyday habits of patients have brought about an imbalance in the body. If the problem is chronic pain, allergies, a respiratory problem, arthritis, difficulty becoming pregnant, and so on, then therapy involves the use of herbal medicine, acupuncture, and occasionally moxibustion, in which *moxa* (mugwort), placed on a sliver of garlic, is burnt on the skin. But physicians switch to a biomedical approach the moment they realize that the patient has an infectious disease, a ruptured spleen, head trauma, or the like, needing urgent attention. Patients will then be referred for tertiary hospital care. In practice, then, a herbal doctor may draw on two completely different sets of ideas about the relationship of nature to nurture while attending to a single patient (Lock 1980).

In isolated parts of the world, people continue to rely on indigenous medical knowledge and practices. In these locales, bodies are usually understood as permeable in one or more ways by forces of many kinds, positive and negative. Anatomical knowledge also varies locally: for example, the alimentary tract can be understood as part of the outside world located inside the body. Living entities – human, animal, and plant – coexist, and non-living entities may be anthropomorphized as part of an animated geography that in turn is subsumed into encompassing supernatural realms. Given that people are increasingly subject to the impact of globalization, indigenous medical thinking is often held in concert with ideas about the body and disease causation introduced from the outside. Nuggets of scientifically based medical knowledge, often about vaccination, antibiotics, and pain-killers, are drawn on alongside indigenous knowledge. Conversely, drug companies in search of plants to patent and convert into patentable drugs value and often exploit indigenous knowledge today.

Of course, even in those countries where biomedicine has been available for decades, pockets of resistance to it remain, one example being families who refuse to have their children vaccinated. Nowhere is everyone willing to discipline the uncertainties of nature, nor does everyone believe that illness is caused by some combination of nature and nurture alone.

Nature, nurture, and the generation of life

European and Arabic thinking about the body was profoundly influenced by Galenism until the mid-nineteenth century, and traces of it remain to this day, as when some of us worry about catching a cold after sitting in a draft. The idea of appropriately situating one's body in the natural world persists, and nurture is enfolded into the cyclical transitions of nature. But ideas about "generation," that is, the creation of life (the term "reproduction" did not come into existence until the mid-eighteenth century) also created debates bearing upon nature and nurture: is the creation of new life a momentary event, written in nature, or a process of development in conjunction with surrounding environments?

The word "*physis*" comes from the same root as plant, in Greek, and in this sense it suggests something emerging gradually, according to a predictable pattern. The image is of a seed producing tiny roots and embryonic leaves that gradually unfold and morph into a mature plant, given the right external circumstances – soil, water, and temperature. In other words, the Greek conception of nature/nurture starts in one form and gradually becomes another while remaining fundamentally unchanged in essence.

In classical Greece, two views of human generation were held. Hippocrates argued that both sexes produce "semen," the intermingling or "blending" of which produced an embryo, and Galen, too, accepted this theory of generation. For Aristotle, on the other hand, semen is the "efficient" cause of generation, and soul, *anima*, is essential for life itself. Aristotle, well aware that menstruation usually ceases at conception, argued that menstrual blood provides the "matter" of the fetus and that the male furnishes its "form" when semen works on female matter.

William Harvey, writing in England in the mid-seventeenth century, and best known for demonstrating the circulation of blood, carried out research on fertilized chicken embryos at different stages of development in order to better understand generation. Up to a point, Harvey followed Aristotelian arguments in that he assumed that semen and menstrual blood are indispensable to the formation and nourishment of embryos. In common with other thinkers of his day, he did not recognize the sexual act as essential to the creation of offspring. But, in striking contrast to Aristotle, he argued that a miniscule, unstructured "pulsating point" of blood is the origin of life (no doubt he came to this conclusion by observing chicken embryos). Harvey insisted that this tiny entity was completely autonomous and must be "developed" by parental nourishment, so that the "work of the father and mother is to be discerned both in the body and the mental character of the offspring" (1847 [1651]: 180). In taking this position, he pushed the origin of life back to a moment prior to that recognized by Aristotle, but, because he makes no direct connection between parents and the actual formation of their offspring, he is left wanting when trying to account for physical resemblances between parents and their children – a matter of great interest to thinkers from classical times.

Harvey concedes that

> the offspring is of a mixed nature, inasmuch as a mixture of both parents appears plainly in it, in the form and lineaments, and each particular part of its body, in its color, mother-marks, disposition to diseases, and other accidents. In mental constitution, also, and its manifestations, such as manners, docility, voice, and gait, a similar temperament is discoverable. (1847 [1651]: 363)

But he also makes it clear that in his opinion:

> The male and female...will come to be regarded as merely the efficient instruments of generation, subservient in all respects to the Supreme Creator, or father of all things. In this sense, consequently, it is well said that the sun and moon engender man....

Harvey's introduction of a Supreme Creator is in striking contrast to the thinking of Greeks and other humoralists. He also wrote that development proceeds as the incremental formation of new entities out of non-structured germ material, similar to the seeds of plants, and it was Harvey who, in the mid-seventeenth century, first used the word "epigenesis" to explain this process. By no means did everyone agree with him, and Jan Swammerdam (1637–80), a pioneer of microscopy, was a severe critic who vehemently opposed Harvey's new idea. Since that time, debates about generation have taken two lines of thought: one, known as preformationism, supported by Swammerdam, assumes that "life" exists in *toto* from the moment of conception; and the other, epigenesis, assumes that the creation of life is a process that continues to unfold gradually over the course of development. As we will see, these competing ideas about the origins of life have waxed and waned over the ensuing centuries. Experiments carried out by Harvey and other researchers established that females of all kinds produce eggs, and Antoni Leeuwenhoek demonstrated the existence of spermatozoa in the second half of the seventeenth century. Even so, arguments persisted among preformationists as to whether the egg or the sperm was the origin of life, and all the while epigenesists continued to voice their position about the importance of unfolding and the contribution of environmental influences. In the seventeenth century, for example, prized horses were imported from Arabia, they usually failed to flourish or reproduce attractive offspring. Many people began to think that the desired features of these horses could be reproduced only if the horses were left in their place of origin. Like Aristotle, breeders defended the idea that local conditions have a decisive role in creating the next generation.

The question as to what brings about resemblances between generations continued to trouble both preformationists and epigenesists. Harvey asked why no "blending" existed in the formation of the two sexes, having noted how rare were hermaphrodites. Accounting for resemblances was made yet more difficult because differences in appearance between twins, siblings, and generations were as readily apparent as were similarities. In 1745, the philosopher/mathematician Maupertuis observed an albino child of black parents. His explanation for this state of affairs was based on Greek ideas known as pangenesis, later taken up by Darwin, namely that generative "particles" exist in all bodily tissues, some of which might occasionally undergo changes. Maupertuis argued that the child's skin and hair color could be due to the particles he or she had inherited from an ancestor, arguing that specific characteristics skip generations. It was years before this prescient insight affected mainstream thinking. Despite early efforts to track families and keep records about resemblances and differences over time, the "epistemic space" of heredity (Müller-Wille and Rheinberger 2012) remained hidden. Aristotle's argument that plant seeds grow differently depending upon the conditions of the soil clearly retained a strong hold on the imagination – and a move to divide and objectify nature and nurture was still a century away.

Until the mid-nineteenth century, contingencies associated with conception, pregnancy, embryonic development, parturition, and lactation were thought to make a contribution to the creation of and to the resemblances apparent in descent generations. It was assumed that likeness was fully accounted for by these many variables, even when striking differences between progenitors and their offspring were recognized. It would take a seismic shift in conceptualization about the origins of life before the concept of "heredity" emerged in a form resembling that familiar to us today. And it would be another century before the molecular mechanism of heredity was finally brought to light.

Evolutionary theory: embracing progress

Enlightenment ideals, to which the idea of progress is central, resulted in a diminishment in the belief that restoration of balance is key to maintaining individual wellbeing. The human body began to be understood as composed of biological units that change diachronically over a lifetime – and over generations through inheritance – on the basis of adaptation to environments. Jean-Baptiste Lamarck, born in Picardy, France, in 1744, is recognized as the first theorist to argue that biological change follows natural laws, although he was not the first to express such thoughts.

Today Lamarck is regarded as a proponent of "soft inheritance theory," an idea that originally had two distinct components. The first, the theory of "use and disuse of body parts" (that increased or decreased use of body parts brings about evolutionary change), is the argument for which Lamarck is most often remembered and ridiculed. The second theory stated that alterations in the environment bring about tiny changes in organisms that are then passed on to ensuing generations. This theory came to be known as the "hereditability of acquired characteristics," and is the reason (as will become clear later) that epigenetics is sometimes described today as neo-Lamarckianism. Lamarck also wrote about a tendency for organisms to become more complex – moving "up" a ladder of progress. In common with many naturalist philosophers of his day, he believed that organisms arose in their simplest forms via spontaneous generation and referred to this phenomenon as "*le pouvoir de la vie*" (the power, or origins, of life) and "*la force qui tend sans cesse à composer l'organisation*" (the force that perpetually tends to make order). He argued that these forces are the basic physical components of biological activity – both of generation, and throughout life. In other words, he took a materialistic approach to biology, and was admired by Charles Darwin for so doing. But Lamarck was not a hardline preformationist and believed, like Darwin, that environments profoundly influence the fundamental force out of which life originates, although, in contrast to Darwin, he did not believe that this process was essentially random.

In 1888, almost sixty years after Lamarck's death, August Weismann, a German evolutionary biologist, conducted an experiment to check the veracity of the French naturalist's claims about inheritance. Weismann removed the tails of numerous white mice repeatedly over five generations and reported that no mice in the following generations were born without a tail or even with a shorter tail. He concluded that Lamarck was wrong. Lamarck's reputation was further sullied in the 1930s when his ideas were adopted by the agriculturalist Trofim Lysenko into the Stalinist regime. Lamarck lived in a time of great political ferment but was fortunate because his work was allowed to proceed unchecked in the herbarium *Le Jardin du Roi*, while the violence of the French Revolution took place on nearby streets. He produced several significant publications influential in his day, but nevertheless was marginalized because he apparently did not believe in God. At the end of his life, Lamarck lost his sight and died in poverty.

Writing in the mid-eighteenth century, Erasmus Darwin, Charles Darwin's extraordinary grandfather, like Lamarck, took a "soft" approach to heredity. Darwin – physician, industrialist, social reformer, and educator of women, among other attributes – wrote several books, in one of which, *The Temple of Nature*, he set out his thoughts on human heredity and disease. Commentators have noted the extent to which the thinking of Lamarck and Erasmus Darwin overlap, although the latter greatly influenced medical reform in his day, unlike the former. Darwin insisted that conditions inherited over generations were not "predestined" by nature, but "predisposed," and argued that heredity is the result of "a malleable admixture of nature and nurture" in which the precipitation of a disease is "triggered" by outside forces (cited in Wilson 2007: 65).

Not surprisingly, Erasmus Darwin was a strong supporter of preventive medicine and argued that individuals must learn how to exert power over nature, and he also became a crusader for social improvement among the working classes. The idea, explicitly asserted by Darwin, and especially his close colleague William Buchan, that behavioral changes and bodily conditions brought about by environments could be carried forward to the embryonic development of the next generation (thus foreshadowing contemporary epigenetics) contributed to the rise of eugenics in Britain. This was so in part because Francis Galton, step-cousin of Charles Darwin, was deeply influenced by their shared grandfather. But Erasmus Darwin and Buchan would both have been hostile to eugenic thinking.

It is not uncommon today to argue that a major shortcoming of a reductionistic approach to healthcare is that the sources of ill health associated with poverty and discrimination are left unexamined, much as was argued in the eighteenth century by Erasmus Darwin and Buchan, who stressed the impact of a negative environment on human wellbeing. But, in the hands of Francis Galton and like-minded thinkers writing in the late nineteenth century, this position stimulated a counter-argument about the innate qualities of degeneracy, decrepitude, and feeblemindedness that should be managed by positive eugenics – that is, by active intervention into human reproduction. Nature was in need of improvement regardless of environment.

From inheritance to heredity

The word "inheritance" was originally used in connection with the transfer of wealth between generations, notably in connection with land. Immanuel Kant's anthropological writings were extremely influential in broadening the idea of inheritance and, in 1788, he created the verb "*vererben*" to signify the "transmission" of biological properties. Kant struggled with the age-old problem of how similarities and differences among humans can be accounted for. Adamant about the unity of the human species, he has been described as promoting "monogenesis" (preformationism). But, because he argued that specific "natural predispositions" in humans, notably skin color, become evident only in certain environments that then attain permanence, he also acknowledges epigenesis. Kant pointed out that Portuguese living in Africa produce white children and, similarly, Africans who settle in Europe have children with dark skin color, regardless of their respective environments (Palsson 2016). He concluded that these dispositions for traits must be present in all humans, are preformed and not acquired, and are transmitted intergenerationally from an original formative force present in all biological matter.

Johann Blumenbach (1752–1840), physician and anthropologist, influenced Kant's thinking about biological inheritance and the tenacity of traits across generations, which contributed greatly in the mid-nineteenth century to the solidification of heredity as a nominal entity. Although "hereditary diseases" had been recognized since antiquity, it was assumed that such conditions were the product of shared environments. Because the mechanism of inheritance remained unknown, such thinking was not readily challenged, and persisted until well into the late eighteenth century, backed by powerful supporters in the medical world.

The noun "*heredité*" was first coined by French doctors in the early part of the nineteenth century, and then taken up in Britain in mid-century. By this time, the majority of concerned medical people, after years of tussling, had been convinced that something resembling a miniscule biological component must be passed consistently from parents to children during the creation of the next generation. For a while there was a wide acceptance of the idea of "blending" or "blended" inheritance, in which characteristics of both parents were thought to meld and average each other out in the next generation.

The path-breaking theory of inheritance by Gregor Mendel was published in 1866, and would eventually put the idea of blended inheritance to rest. As is well known, Mendel, an Augustinian monk, worked with several characteristics of pea plants. With respect to seed color, for example, he showed that when a yellow pea and a green pea are bred together, their offspring is always yellow (not, as blended inheritance might suggest, a yellowy-green color). However, in the next generation, the green color reappears in a ratio of one to three. Mendel coined the terms "recessive" and "dominant" to express what he had observed. After its publication, this extraordinary finding remained largely unnoticed; the paper was assumed to be about hybridization rather than inheritance, and was cited only three or four times over the next thirty-five years. Apparently Mendel did not understand the significance of his own findings; only at the dawn of the twentieth century did the budding discipline of genetics discredit blended inheritance by asserting that characteristics are dominantly or recessively inherited, as Mendel had shown.

Once rediscovered in 1900, Mendel's findings gave irrefutable backing to a dawning realization of the day that a "particulate theory" would best account for the transmission of life-giving entities between generations. Such a theory, entertained since the time of the Greeks, had been self-consciously resuscitated and adopted in modified form in the mid-nineteenth century by

Charles Darwin, whose thinking was profoundly influenced by his own research into animal and plant breeding. Darwin, of course, devoted his life's work to demonstrating how living entities of all kinds respond to environmental variables that impinge upon them. He proposed that certain effects from the environment might become embodied in an individual's constitution and then be transmitted to the next generation via entities he called "gemmules" that enter the germ cells (gametes). Darwin, giving a nod to the Greeks, argued that cells alone could generate new tissues and new organisms – both processes set in motion by the "shedding" of gemmules. Some gemmules, he asserted, remain dormant for generations, whereas others are active in ensuing generations. Darwin likened this process to gardening, a flowerbed sprinkled with seeds, many of which perish while others germinate.

Gemmules are often described today as precursors of genes, that is, of modern preformationism, and although this may be accurate to the extent that Darwin was struggling to find molecular particles involved in the creation of life, equally he had in mind a process resembling the contemporary theory of "epigenetic inheritance," in which modifications in DNA that take place during the lifetime of an individual can, at times, be passed on to ensuing generations. Reciprocally, epigenetic inheritance, on occasion labeled as "soft inheritance," is a term applied retroactively to Darwin's thinking. Darwin would certainly have taken issue with Social Darwinians of today who, originally influenced by Herbert Spencer (1820–1903), are vocal advocates of genetic determinism (hard inheritance). Darwin thought of the contributions made by nurture to heredity as context-dependent and fluid; he conceptualized living entities as subject to environmental forces able to bring about lasting changes, random in origin. Darwin's theory of "descent with modification" suggests that he was a proponent of a randomized "epigenesis" – William Harvey's concept used consistently until the end of the nineteenth century as a gloss for "nurture" or "environment."

Darwin breaks entirely with the synchronic thinking characteristic of humoralism, in which changes to human bodies are accounted for by alterations in environmental forces, many of which are seasonally based. In contrast, Darwin gives precedence to diachronic change that accrues in populations of living entities over time. His theorizing is post-Enlightenment, even though, in his own words, he is far from enamored with an innate idea of "progress," and is committed to a minute investigation of biological change in individuals and their adaptive qualities over time in populations. Darwin consciously opted to stay away from politics, and dreaded the confrontations he was forced to endure because his theory of evolution had no need of God. He supported Lamarck in his belief in the inheritance of acquired characteristics, but, being first and foremost a scientist, Darwin was in search of a mechanism of inheritance, although he was the first to agree that his proposed idea about gemmules was probably too complex.

Herbert Spencer postulated a theory of evolution before Darwin which was all-embracing, and integrated the progressive development of the physical world and biological organisms, the human mind, human culture, and societies. He explicitly compared society to a living organism. It was Spencer who, after reading Darwin's *On the Origin of Species* (1859), created the idiom "survival of the fittest." Spencer drew parallels between his ideas about social evolution and Darwin's writing: "This survival of the fittest, which I have here sought to express in mechanical terms, is that which Mr Darwin has called 'natural selection', or the preservation of favored races in the struggle for life" (Spencer 1864: 444–5).

Spencer and Darwin corresponded, and it is clear that Darwin not only agreed with Spencer's idiom, but also believed it to be more accurate than his own concept of natural selection, even though Spencer, unlike Darwin, insisted that evolution would reach an equilibrated endpoint. Darwin died over twenty years before Spencer, who lived until 1903, by which time he was frequently characterized as an ultra-conservative. Spencer attempted to introduce the theories of Lamarck and Darwin into sociological theorizing of his day – efforts that were actively rejected by some.

In sum, knowledge accruing in the early modern period from several different sources strongly suggested that the mystery of generation – the transmission of specific characteristics from one generation to the next – must, through some random process, be accomplished during reproduction by particulate matter. Consolidation of these ideas was influenced by systematic animal and plant breeding in which efforts were made with considerable success to re-create desired characteristics in ensuing generations, a practice to which Charles Darwin contributed; the creation of plant taxonomies, notably that of Linneaus, based on systematic classification of the external characteristics of plants; the formation of a classification of human diseases in the medical world; experiments that attempted to overturn the concept of preformation; and a mounting interest in the discipline of physical anthropology in skin color changes over generations where mixed unions had taken place between the so-called "races."

The cumulative evidence furnished by these respective domains resulted in the early twentieth-century recognition of a new conceptual space – a notion of heredity with a focus on "elementary traits or dispositions independent of the particular life forms of which they were a part, whether pathological or normal, maternal or paternal, individual or specific" (Müller-Wille and Rheinberger 2007: 13). This theory of heredity, in contrast to thinking throughout much of the latter part of the twentieth century, in which genes were regarded as the source of life itself, was depicted as a generalized phenomenon – the key to reproduction and an explanation for similarities so visible across generations. The majority of scientists directly involved in bringing about this singular shift in thinking thoroughly excoriated beliefs about preformationism, homunculi, and the contribution of supernatural forces to generation, but these ideas were not laid to rest for ever, as we will see.

TWO

Promotion and Demotion of the Gene

Mechanisms of inheritance

In the latter part of the nineteenth century, inheritance was often thought of as the transmission of a force, or vital property, that could be "strong" or "weak," as were the laws of physics. But where, exactly, were these vital entities – these units of heredity – to be found? What is more, the appearance of either similar or dissimilar features in ensuing generations could not be accounted for satisfactorily by scientists of the day, despite experimental investigation. This chapter is about the long struggle to isolate and pin down a natural "force" that generates new life in humans and other animate entities, culminating in the recognition of the chemical structure of DNA and, several decades later, the mapping of the human genome.

As noted in the previous chapter, Charles Darwin's 1868 effort to conceptualize the missing vital force was to postulate the existence of "gemmules," an effort not well received by many of his contemporaries. Two years earlier, Gregor Mendel had referred to invisible "*Faktoren*" (factors), and in the final decades of the nineteenth century a dozen or more other terms came into use, among the most influential being "stirp," adopted by Francis Galton in 1876, which he explicitly distinguished from gemmules. In 1884, Carl Nagelli, a Swiss botanist who worked on cell division, invented the word "idioplasm"; in 1889, Hugo de Vries, a Dutch botanist, modified Darwin's term to that of "intracellular pangenes'"; and at the turn of the twentieth century, August Weismann made use of the terms "biophores" and "determinants." It was clearly a time fermenting with ideas about miniature forces with the power to produce new life.

In England, Herbert Spencer, in 1863, was the first to adopt the concept of "heredity," originally postulated in France in the 1820s following years of vituperative debate, and Francis Galton soon followed him. Galton and Spencer met for occasional chats and games of billiards at their shared London club. Both men were actively opposed to organized religion, and each, in his own way, consigned Darwin's theory of natural selection to the margins. Galton set out to prove or disprove once and for all Darwin's theory of pangenesis by performing an ingenious series of experiments on rabbits to see if blood transfusions would alter heritable characteristics. He mixed the blood taken from gray rabbits with that of white rabbits, thereby blending their respective "gemmules," and then re-infused the mixture into all the rabbits. If gemmules functioned as Darwin claimed, then the next generation should be mongrels, but this was not the case – the offspring all had gray fur. Galton concluded that the function of gemmules, if indeed they existed, was of relatively minor importance.

Galton confined his own particulate concept, "stirp" (derived from *stirpes*, a root), to the ovum. He argued that "the whole of the 'stirp', together with much of mere nutriment, is packed into a space not exceeding the size of the head of a pin." Galton laments that one cannot really see the ovum, even with a microscope, but concludes:

> Ova and their contents are…much what mail-bags and the heaps of letters poured out of them are to those who gaze through the glass windows of a post office. Such persons may draw various valuable conclusions as to the postal communications generally, but they cannot read a single word of what the letters contain. All that we may learn concerning the constituents of the stirp must be through inference, and not by direct observation. (Galton 1876: 331)

Galton explicitly argued that hereditable characteristics are not transmitted throughout the body in the blood, as he claimed Darwin had suggested. (Darwin refuted this.) He stressed the importance of "double parentage" for complex organisms, and argued that both parents contribute equally to succeeding generations. He, like Darwin, apparently accepted the idea of blended inheritance. Galton came close to rediscovering Mendel's particulate theory of inheritance when he posited that, at fertilization, half the stirps from each parent must be "suppressed," thus accounting for similarities and differences in ensuing generations, and for the fact that certain obvious diseases "skip" generations.

Galton argued that a complete theory of heredity should be "divided into two groups," one that refers to "inborn or congenital peculiarities that were also congenital in one or more ancestors," and another composed of characteristics "acquired for the first time...during their lifetime, owing to some change in the conditions of their life." He insisted that the first of these groups is of singular importance because these "inborn" characteristics are readily explainable in a "broad and general way" by more than one theory. With respect to the second group, the evidence is difficult to verify, and should be regarded, he suggested, contra Darwin, as "supplementary and subordinate" to the first (Galton 1876: 330).

Galton's partiality to eugenic thinking becomes apparent when he writes: "We may compare the stirp to a nation, and those among its germs that achieve development, to the foremost men of a nation who succeed in becoming its representatives." But he nevertheless concludes that "the law of heredity goes no further than to say, that like *tends* to produce like; the tendency may be very strong but it cannot be absolute" (Galton 1876: 330; emphasis added). Even so, Galton tips the scales heavily towards "nature" and, in contrast to Darwin, takes what came to be called a "hard view of heredity."

August Weismann acknowledged Galton's position on reproduction as contributory to his thinking, but his investigations brought about new insights. In common with other biologists, Weismann struggled with irresolvable oppositions evident in his day between theories of creationism and evolution. Influenced by Darwin, he supported evolutionary theory strongly, but he changed his opinion about the mechanism of inheritance several times over the course of his life. Identified by advances in German lens production, chromosomes were demonstrated and recognized as vectors of heredity in the mid-1880s, a finding that was at first hotly contested. Furthermore, cytologists became aware of the processes of mitosis and meiosis associated with cell division at this time but, prior to Weismann, they did not understand their significance.

Weismann's delicate research with sea urchin embryos suggested that multi-cellular organisms must be made up of two kinds of cells: germ cells, which contain heritable information, and somatic cells, which perform bodily functions. Weismann argued that germ cells, with their stored germ-plasm, are not influenced by the environment, by learning, or by morphological changes that happen during the lifetime of an organism, hence soma-to-germline feedback is impossible. Furthermore, germ cells are "held in trust for coming generations." Weismann also recognized that when reproduction takes place, "diploid" cells must divide twice to produce four "haploid cells" if the number of chromosomes is to remain the same. His theory of heredity, published in the late 1880s, became known as the Weismannian Barrier, marking the end of the long history of epigenesis formulated by William Harvey in the seventeenth century. This theory opened the door wide to genetic determinism – the idea that our genes define who we are; a molecularized preformationism. Although Galton followed these developments closely, his interests were broader. He became preoccupied with evolution on a grand scale and, above all, how best to influence breeding among the human race.

Biometrics and the elimination of degeneracy

> *[C]haracter, including the aptitude for work, is heritable
> like every other faculty.*
>> Francis Galton, *Memories of My Life*, 1908

Galton used the term "eugenics" for the first time in
1883. He made it clear that improvement of the "stock"
of the human race was desirable, and had in mind a
breeding program similar to that already in widespread
use in animal husbandry. In the introduction to
Inquiries into Human Faculty and Its Development, he
comments:

> We must free our minds of a great deal of prejudice
> before we can rightly judge of the direction in which
> different races need to be improved. We must be on
> our guard against taking our own instincts of what is
> best and most seemly, as a criterion for the rest of
> mankind. The instincts and faculties of different men
> and races differ in a variety of ways almost as pro-
> foundly as those of animals in different cages of the
> Zoological Gardens.... The moral and intellectual
> wealth of a nation largely consists in the multifarious
> variety of the gifts of the men who compose it, and
> it would be the very reverse of improvement to
> make all its members assimilate to a common type.

> However, . . . in the rapidly changing race of man,
> there are elements, some ancestral and others the result
> of degeneration, that are of little or no value, or are
> positively harmful. (Galton 1883: 1–2)

For Galton, uncovering the mechanism of heredity was
not a driving ambition, and he was well aware that a
successful program of eugenics must be grounded
in inferences based on large populations of individuals, preferably over more than one generation. His
primary objective was to demonstrate a probabilistic
relationship between the features of an organism and
the features of its offspring. Galton was a talented math-
ematician, became the founding figure of a field of
inquiry known as "biometrics," and was one of the
founding editors in 1901 of the journal *Biometrika*.

The historian Ruth Schwartz Cowan (1972b) describes
Galton as a compulsive "counter and measurer." She cites
a letter that he wrote to his brother reporting that he had
made measurements of Hottentot women while traveling
in South Africa:

> I have dexterously even without the knowledge of
> the parties concerned, resorted to actual measure-
> ment. . . . I sat at a distance with my sextant, and as the
> ladies turned themselves about, as women always do,
> to be admired, I surveyed them in every way and

subsequently...worked out and tabulated the results at my leisure. (Cowan 1972b: 510)

Following his travels, Galton settled down to his primary quest of improving the mental abilities of "mankind," but he would have to overcome resistance from theologians and many scientists of the day who were strong supporters for improving the environment – of enhancing nurture, rather than manipulating nature.

Galton established a research program to investigate human variation in connection with human ability, height, facial images, and fingerprint patterns, with the purpose of establishing which of these features are inherited. He researched both identical and non-identical twins to ascertain whether those dissimilar at birth converged when reared in similar environments. He concluded that nature rather than nurture was decisive. He also experimented with sweet peas, completely unaware of Mendel's work. He sent packets of weighed sweet peas to seven of his friends, and asked them to grow them and then return the daughter seeds to him. He noted that the seeds of the daughter plants, however variable the parent seed in weight, "reverted" to a mean weight. He collected another set of data on the physiques of boys in town and country schools for comparative purposes, but his largest body of information came from an Anthropometric Laboratory he built, using his own income, in the International Health Exhibition at the Science Museum in South Kensington in 1885. Well over 9,000 people, including many parents and their offspring, were measured in this laboratory. Galton charged each person a token amount, and collected data on height, weight, breathing power, strength of pull, hearing, and sight, among other measurements.

The mathematical insights of the Belgian Astronomer-Royal, Adolphe Quetelet, inspired Galton when he used the concept of the normal bell curve to demonstrate how the many variables he had observed are distributed around a mean. He formulated the idea of regression from a mean, a concept used in statistics today, and set out the principles of correlation, with Pearson, examples of which appear daily in the media when we are reminded that eating junk food puts us at risk for many ills, and that smoking causes cancer. Galton also deduced that children who deviate greatly from their parents in physical appearance are "sports," that is, they exhibit one or more "mutations."

Galton located the phenomenon of heredity equally in the physical appearance of individuals and in that of populations, because "all that a population possesses (in the biological sense) it possesses by virtue of heredity" (cited in Cowan 1972a: 408). For Galton, the "force" of heredity could be measured by outward appearances alone. On the other hand, behaviors and conditions such as drunkenness and insanity are not inherited consistently in populations, and hence, he deduced, these variables must be the work of "nurture," that is, of bad parenting. Galton did not, however, go so far as to argue that eugenic policies should be implemented, and was explicitly opposed to government coercion.

From positive to negative eugenics

Galton died in 1911, by which time the word "heredity" was in wide usage, and with it came a marked division in the minds of both scientists and the public between "nature" and "nurture" – heredity and environment. Oxford and Cambridge universities had both awarded Galton an honorary degree, he received the Huxley Gold Medal of the Anthropological Institute, and was ultimately knighted. In 1906, he delivered the annual Herbert Spencer Lecture, at which he gave a talk titled: "Probability – The Foundation of Eugenics." Galton was the founding president of the Eugenics Education Society, opened in London in 1907, with the aim of promoting research in connection with the "improvement" of the population.

The legacy for which Galton is undoubtedly best remembered is that of eugenics, but his goal and that of his colleagues was limited to a scientific demonstration of the driving force of heredity using biometrics to assess the distribution of mental-, physical-, and health-related characteristics in populations. Applied, "positive eugenics" took off following Galton's death when several government initiatives were set up in the United States and Europe to encourage people to emulate those families deemed by officials to be particularly healthy in mind and body.

Charles Davenport, an American biologist, devoted his time to the creation and collection of family pedigrees. He took a position more extreme than that of Galton when he observed that "pauperism," "criminality," and especially "feeble-mindedness" are heritable, and went on to argue that individuals with such traits should be prohibited from reproducing so that "defective protoplasm" might be eliminated from the gene pool, a practice described as negative eugenics. Davenport proclaimed: "Prevent the feeble minded, drunkards, paupers, sex offenders, and criminalistic from marrying their like or cousins or any person belonging to a neuropathic strain" (Davenport 1910: 12).

Davenport attempted to develop a quantitative approach to human miscegenation, and provided what he described as statistical evidence for "biological and cultural degradation" following "interbreeding between white and black populations" (cited in Gillette 2007: 123–4). The Harvard geneticist E.M. East (1917) recommended that whole families should be put under surveillance; a matter of urgency he claimed, because "civilized" societies permit the numbers of "defective" people to increase by means of medicine and charities that interfere with natural selection. Comments such as these were well publicized, and thousands of Americans gave financial support to the activities of the Eugenics Record Office in Cold Spring Harbor, of which Davenport was director. The Eugenics Record Office repeatedly provided a scientific rationale for growing anti-immigrant sentiments in the United States, signaling warnings to immigration authorities at Ellis Island, New York, where many passengers were "processed," no less than 1.25 million passengers in the record year of 1907. Any outward sign of illness might mean careful inspection and deportation. Ellis Island, the island of hope, the gate to the New World, was thus also dubbed the "Island of Tears."

Eugenics was transformed rapidly in the early part of the twentieth century from a rather obscure science into a major political movement in which applied eugenics would be used to purge populations of "unwanted degeneracy" by making sterilization compulsory. Many staunch supporters of eugenics were progressive-minded social thinkers including Emma Goldman, George Bernard Shaw, H.G. Wells, and Margaret Sanger. Among these writers and activists, the eugenics movement was recognized not only as a means to improve the biological stock of nations, but also as a foundation for social reform. Margaret Sanger wrote: "Those least fit to carry on the race are increasing most rapidly.... Funds that should be used to raise the standard of our civilization are diverted to the maintenance of those who should never have been born" (1922: 98). Nobel Prize winner Konrad Lorenz, a member of the Nazi Party and its Office for Race Policy, was inspired by Friedrich Nietzsche's explicit equation between the civilization of humans and the domestication of animals. In 1940, Lorenz advocated a program of eugenics in which "ethically inferior people" would be exterminated, and children born of mixed marriages between Germans and Poles deemed genetically deficient would be sent to concentration camps.

The eugenics movement, supported by many geneticists, grew stronger during the Depression, and research into diabetes, epilepsy, syphilis, "feeble-mindedness," and other diseases was motivated not merely by an interest to discover the mechanism of the diseases, but also by a concern about their financial burden on society. In the United States, it is estimated that 50,000 individuals were forcibly sterilized during the first half of the twentieth century. This practice was replicated in Canada, South Africa, and across northern Europe, including the social-democratic countries of Scandinavia, with Germany being by far the most extreme. Lawsuits continue to the present day in connection with these practices, which persisted in Sweden, Canada, and elsewhere until the 1970s and after. A report published in 2013 revealed that at least 148 women had been sterilized involuntarily in California between 2006 and 2010. Similar programs were implemented in Japan and China in the late nineteenth century, where, as was the case in Europe, intellectuals spearheaded compulsory sterilization. Such practices became illegal in the 1990s in Japan, but in China they continued and morphed into the infamous one-child policy established in the late 1970s. India had a forced sterilization program under Indira Gandhi in which lower-caste males were the primary targets, and today unscrupulous sterilization practices of poor women persist throughout the country.

The gene and modern preformationism

Galton's work on inheritance had a second impact that often goes unnoticed, namely, stimulating research by cell biologists. One result was that in 1900 Mendel's laws of inheritance were brought to light again, thereby paving the way for modern genetics. William Bateson coined the term "genetics" in 1906, and three years later the Danish plant physiologist Wilhelm Johannsen, who was also the first to make a distinction between genotype (which we would today define as the set of genes responsible for a particular trait) and phenotype (the physical expression of such a trait), introduced the word "gene." Johannsen argued that a genotype results from nothing but the egg and the sperm that fertilizes it, whereas the phenotype develops from a seed, or an egg, at a later stage in development. The actual phenomenon of heredity is found in the genotype alone, he insisted, an entity composed of genes that have different forms known as alleles.

Johannsen was at pains to dispose of preformationism and its associated animism. He and others disagreed adamantly with Weismann's ideas about particulate "biophores" that determine life; they argued that the concept "gene" would be a more accurate characterization than Weismann's because it stood up to experimentation. Johannsen, who likened the new genetics to the "hard" science of chemistry, also dismissed outright the law of ancestral inheritance accepted by Darwin, Weismann, and others. His arguments created a marked distinction between the transmission of hereditary factors, accomplished by genes alone, and characteristics resulting from embryonic development. The chemist H.E. Armstrong wrote in the 1930s that biography will eventually be written in terms of structural chemistry, and descent explained in terms of the permutations and combinations brought about by genes alone. Thus was the stage set for an era that came to be dominated by genetic determinism, consolidated by the mid-twentieth-century discovery of the structure of DNA – irrefutable evidence, it was assumed, of the units of inheritance and the origin of life itself.

But certain scientists, notably in the United States, remained uncomfortable about the implications of particulate theorizing. The zoologist Thomas Hunt Morgan argued:

> The original conception of praeformation postulated an actual material embryo in the egg; epigenesis denied the existence of that embryo, and justified its denial.... We no longer look for an actual embryo praeformed, but we look for samples of each part,

which samples by increasing in size and joining suitably to other parts make the embryo. This is modern praeformation. (1910: 452)

Despite this initial reaction, Morgan delved into genetics, his thinking influenced by his student Hermann J. Muller, who published a highly influential paper in which he argued explicitly that the secrets common to all life lie in genetic material alone (Muller 1951 [1926]). The term "gene action" came into use at this time, although the idea of the gene itself remained very fuzzy, and its functions – actions – could not be spelled out. There were two functions that had to be explained, and they were contradictory: first, to account for what determines the properties of an organism so that it is reliably replicated; and, second, to account for Mendelian patterns of inheritance involving variation and difference. Evelyn Fox Keller notes that the early twentieth-century idea of the gene "offers a resolution of the riddle of life *by invoking an entity that is a riddle in and of itself*" (2002: 131; emphasis added). The gene had to subsume internal incoherence that could not be explained and so it was left, in effect, as a black box.

Morgan made a significant contribution to solving the riddle when in 1934 he noted that an assumption of his day was that all genes act all the time in the same way. He postulated, in contrast, that different batteries of genes come into operation at different times as development proceeds, and noted that this process appears to be initiated in the protoplasm of the egg. Here is the first explicit vision of cell differentiation in human development, and Morgan argued explicitly that genes could not be the only agents involved.

In 1943, Erwin Schrödinger, best known as the "father" of quantum mechanics, gave a series of lectures in Dublin, a city to which he was exiled for the duration of the war. The lectures were published in book form under the title *What Is Life?*, which Richard Lewontin (1992) later described as an "ideological manifesto of the new biology." Schrödinger was grappling with a contradiction that he perceived between physics and biology. The second law of thermodynamics states that entropy (a measure of disorder) inevitably increases, whereas the existence of a "genetic memory" in living entities apparently not only persists throughout the lifetime of individuals, but is "immortal," and transmitted to succeeding generations. Schrödinger argued that the structure of the chromosomes must be responsible for keeping biological entities alive and must contain "some kind of code-script," but he concluded:

[T]he term code-script is, of course, too narrow. The
chromosome structures are at the same time instru-
mental in bringing about the development they fore-
shadow. They are law-code and executive power – or,
to use another simile, they are architect's plan and
builder's craft – in one. (2006 [1944]: 22–3)

Schrödinger's arguments were congruent with similar
developments taking place more generally in the biological sciences, to which many physicists and chemists
of the day contributed, and his publications provided
enormous impetus for the molecularization of Mendelian genetics. An epigraph to one of Schrödinger's
chapters is *Cogito ergo sum* ("I think therefore I am"),
but Evelyn Fox Keller argues that for Schrödinger, in
contrast to Descartes, "self is not in the pineal gland
but... in the molecular structure of the gene." It is there
that can be found the "signalman, a little man within
a man, who makes the apparatus tick." Keller concludes
that this particular concept of the gene is "Janus-faced:
part physicist's atom and part Platonic soul – at one and
the same time a fundamental building block and an
animating force" (1996: 9–10). Schrödinger renamed
the gene as a "device," such that every cell of the body
contains a repetition of the code-script, somewhat akin

to a computer program: a preformed message that survives the death of individuals, to be passed on to following generations.

The Code of Codes

Common knowledge has it that DNA was discovered in the 1950s by the physicist Francis Crick and the molecular biologist James Watson. The well-known Cambridge pub "The Eagle" proclaims that this is so on one of its walls, but this is not the case. DNA was first identified in the late 1860s by a Swiss chemist, Friedrich Miescher, while searching for proteins in white blood cells. During the course of his experiments, he found a substance in the nuclei of the blood cells that was unlike any protein known to him. Miescher gave this material the name of nuclein, which was changed over the years first to nucleic acid, and then to deoxyribonucleic acid (DNA). Miescher's finding fell into obscurity until the first decade of the twentieth century; only in 1944 did Oswald Avery and his colleagues at Rockefeller University demonstrate that hereditary material is composed of DNA. An Austrian biochemist, Erwin Chargaff, inspired by this finding, decided to experiment with samples of DNA taken from many species. He reported in 1950 that nucleotide sequences vary considerably among species but, nevertheless, all organisms share in common the basic properties of DNA. Furthermore, he showed that the nucleotides of which DNA is composed come in four forms: guanine (G), adenine (A), thymine (T), and cytosine (C). Chargaff's remarkable insight was to recognize that the respective amounts of G to A and of C to T in DNA are essentially the same, thus beginning to explain how DNA replicates itself.

In an extremely short paper published in *Nature* in 1953, titled "A Structure for Deoxyribose Nucleic Acid," Crick and Watson cite Chargaff but not Miescher or, more surprisingly, Avery. They emphasize the provisional nature of their findings, and make clear the shortcomings of Linus Pauling's previous attempt to elucidate DNA structure. The penultimate sentence is memorable for its uncharacteristic cautiousness: "It has not escaped our notice that the specific pairing we have postulated [of G with A and T with C] immediately suggests a possible copying mechanism for the genetic material" (Crick and Watson 1953: 737). The editors of *Nature* had agreed ahead of time to publish in the same issue two more articles related to the work of Crick and Watson: the first detailed the X-ray crystallography findings of DNA carried out by the team of

Maurice Wilkins; and the second described the work of a group headed up by Rosalind Franklin, in which the crystallography identified the helical, three-dimensional structure of DNA. Crick and Watson state in their paper that they had been "stimulated" prior to their publication by the findings of the X-ray crystallographers, but the task remained for them to spell out the precise structure of the helical chains – to affirm, crucially, that these chains run in opposite directions, and hence are able to chemically uncouple and re-couple. Crick, Watson, and Maurice Wilkins received the Nobel Prize in 1962 for this work, which overwhelmingly added weight to supporters of genetic determinism. Rosalind Franklin died in 1958 and the Nobel cannot be awarded posthumously; even so, her omission as one of the recipients has been widely criticized.

The work of the French geneticists François Jacob and Jacques Monod and colleagues uncovered the role of messenger RNA (mRNA) in 1960. Then, in 1970, elaborating on an argument first set out in 1956, Francis Crick published a paper in *Nature* titled "Central Dogma of Molecular Biology," describing how coding sequence specificity is accomplished: DNA is first transcribed into RNA, which then specifies the sequence of amino acids constituting the resultant proteins. This formula is often glossed, even in textbooks today, as DNA makes RNA makes protein – an over-simplification that massively understates the complexity involved but which set in place what has come to be known universally as a "genetic program." The ambiguities persisted, however: are genes the initial activators of life? Are they controllers and regulators or are they acted upon by something else that then permits genes to become activators? What *is* accepted is that the instructions for development of organisms are encoded in the computer-like digital sequences of nucleotide bases – this becomes the new *telos* for life itself.

A vision of the Grail

By the mid-1980s, discussions were under way about mapping the entire human genome. A prominent advocate, Walter Gilbert, a Harvard physicist who switched to molecular biology, was not alone in arguing that undertaking such a project was the "biological grail." This endeavor, he insisted, would tell us what it is that makes us human; explain how a human develops from an egg; and inform us about biological variation across the species (Gilbert 1992: 84). Carrying out the project was essential, Gilbert argued, because once the sequence of the genome is known, scientists would have a powerful research tool – the blueprint for life itself.

In 1990, the Human Genome Project (HGP) was officially launched with an audacious plan to complete a full sequence in fifteen years. Over 2,000 scientists from more than twenty institutes located in six countries were commissioned to produce the first "working draft." Much of the work was divided up, and teams were often awarded a specific chromosome on which to work. In 1997, UNESCO set out a Universal Declaration on the Human Genome and Human Rights: "The human genome underlines the fundamental unity of all members of the human family, as well as the recognition of their inherent dignity and diversity. In a symbolic sense, it is the heritage of humanity." By 2001, it was announced that the Project was close to completion, and the 3.08 billion base pairs of the DNA that comprise the genome of *Homo sapiens* had largely been mapped, a feat compared to the Apollo moon landing. Two teams, numbering over 200 scientists, published their findings, the first, which was publicly funded, in *Nature*, and the second, a privately funded project, in *Science*.

The *Nature* issue (490, 11, 2012) included a wall chart of the new "universe within":

> Since ancient times we have drawn charts of the sky,
> of the world, and of our anatomy. Today, a new chart
> is added to the collection.... We invite you on a tour
> of the geography of the genome, exploring the chro-
> mosomes, the sequences, and the differences between
> individuals and populations... these exciting new find-
> ings usher in a new era of scientific and medical
> progress.

One journalist reported that mapping the genome "was
like [completing] God's own jigsaw puzzle" (Hall 2013).
But a good number of commentators mixed excitement
with caution. Nobel laureate David Baltimore wrote:

> I've seen a lot of exciting biology emerge over the past
> 40 years. But chills still ran down my spine when I first
> read the paper that describes the outline of our
> genome.... Not that many questions are definitively
> answered – for conceptual impact, it does not hold a
> candle to Watson and Crick's 1953 paper describing
> the structure of DNA. (2001: 814)

Baltimore intimated that we need no longer ask "What
makes us human?" but that the abiding question:
"What differentiates one organism from another?" had
come to the fore (2001: 816). His comment brings
environment – nurture – to center stage. Other, less

sanguine commentators noted that the map resembled a list of parts for a Boeing 747, but with no idea as to how the parts go together and no knowledge of the principles of aeronautics. Gene ambiguity is first disambiguated and then immediately re-created, demanding new investigations.

Thousands of human genomes have now been sequenced, as have those of numerous other species. The data are used worldwide in the biomedical sciences, anthropology, forensics, and evolutionary biology. National genetic databases designed to systematically examine the genetic makeup of whole populations have proved to be informative about centuries-old human migrations and also assist in promoting preventive healthcare.

Certain researchers in molecular and cell biology, developmental biology, and population genetics had been critical prior to the HGP of the genetic determinism it was likely to foster. They based their critique on knowledge in their respective fields available in the 1970s. The cell biologist Richard Strohman insisted that "there *is* no program in the sense of an inherited, preexisting script waiting to be read." Rather, he argued, "there are regulatory networks of proteins that sense or measure changes in the cellular environment and interpret those signals so that the cell makes an appropriate response" (2001: 6). This dynamic epige-netic network has a "life of its own," and is a context-dependent reactive system of which DNA is just one part. Thus, contingency displaces determinism. But most biologists paid little attention to Strohman's insights, and the dogma of genetic determinism remained essentially unscathed.

Technologies that enabled rapid DNA analysis per-mitted a massive redeployment of agency and morality to the gene. Increasingly, DNA evidence is used as the irrefutable mark of individual identity, whether in the courtroom as forensic evidence, or to determine if a female athlete is really what she claims to be. Our biog-raphies are written today, in part, in terms of structural chemistry: traces of DNA can determine, with consid-erable certainty, whether an individual was present or not when a particular event took place, and DNA anal-yses are routinely used to verify the remains of people who have "disappeared," as in the Argentinean Dirty War, the war in Kosovo, and mass drug warfare killings in Mexico. Similarly, by conflating sex, gender, and genes, it is assumed that a person's identity as a woman or man can be "truthfully" ascertained on the basis of DNA testing. Chemical identities are preformationist creations, to which environmental and social variables make no contribution.

Genomic surprises

Research started to dethrone the deterministic gene even before the HGP commenced – in 1968, it was found that large amounts of DNA sequences are repetitive, the reason for their existence not understood. Following the HGP, the idea that genes determine life has taken a severe beating. A complex landscape of over 3.2 billion DNA base pairs was revealed and one guesstimate was that the entire sequence could stretch to the moon and back 150,000 times. Practically every cell in the adult human body contains a copy of the human genome, one of two kinds: the nuclear genome – divided into twenty-four linear chromosomes – and the mitochondrial genome (mtDNA) – a circular DNA molecule of 16,569 nucleotides composed largely of the DNA of bacteria that long ago lost the ability to live independently. In addition to this startling finding, the genomes in each of the cells of our bodies are not all the same, owing to epigenetic activity.

DNA is inert, a remarkable insight that has been known for many years. As Richard Lewontin put it:

DNA is...among the most nonreactive chemically inert molecules in the world...[it] has no power to reproduce itself. Rather it is produced out of elementary materials by a complex machinery of proteins. While it is often said that DNA produces proteins, in fact proteins (enzymes) produce DNA. The newly manufactured DNA is certainly a copy of the old...but we do not describe the Eastman Kodak factory as a place of self-reproduction [of photographs].

He continues:

[T]he proteins of the cell are made by other proteins and without that protein-forming machinery *nothing* can be made...an egg, before fertilization, contains a complete apparatus of production deposited there in the course of its cellular development. We inherit not only genes made of DNA but an intricate structure of cellular machinery made up of proteins. (Lewontin 1992: 33)

In sum, human development, like that of all other organisms, is not accomplished as a result of a genetic "program" – genes do not *cause* development, but are activated by other parts of the genome responding to signals external and internal to the organism and its cells. Networks of interacting proteins are widely understood as self-organized and not as part of a pre-encoded program. The production of biological stability is not intrinsic to DNA; this is achieved through the agency of systems of enzymes and DNA sequences regulated by many elements, both inside and outside the genome, that together determine when and to what extent sequences will be activated. Moreover, genes do not have clearly demarcated beginnings and ends and, among their sub-specialties, geneticists demarcate genes differently.

There is further complexity: at times during reproduction, deletions or transpositions of elements take place. Specific genes are "silenced" largely by epigenetic modifications, or are repeated many times, among yet other changes. The redundancy evident in the genome is assumed to ensure that, regardless of molecular mistakes (of which there are many) and whatever environmental contingencies are encountered, biological development can, with some exceptions, take place successfully. Mapping the human genome – the vaunted project of genetic determinists – consolidated the above knowledge, which proved very problematic for the simple equation of the genome as the code for life, much of which had been intuited by some scientists before the Holy Grail loomed on the horizon.

It was formerly thought that the genome is composed entirely of genes that code for proteins, but this was yet another assumption that some scientists had long suspected could not be the case. The HGP revealed that genes that code for proteins are unevenly distributed on chromosomes, clustering at particular sites. Furthermore, among these genes, many code for more than one protein, and sometimes many. It was revealed that humans have approximately 20,000 genes, and not 100,000 as had been predicted. Numerous plants have many more genes than do humans, and the diminutive worm *C. elegans* has about the same number as ourselves. Furthermore, the similarities of the human genome to those of other living organisms are closer than was expected. As Charles Darwin surmised, we are evolutionarily close to the great apes, and share approximately 99% of our DNA with chimpanzees and bonobos. (Certain experts argue that 90% is more accurate.) But we also share about 35% of our DNA with daffodils, although – crucially – such figures mean little because they tell us nothing about the *circumstances under which genes are expressed*, or, indeed, if they are expressed at all.

It is recognized today that the size of a genome bears no relationship to its complexity, and that the genome is not equivalent to the organism: "The role of the genome has been turned on its head," Evelyn Fox Keller argues, "transforming it from an executive suite of directional instructions to an exquisitely sensitive...system that enables cells to regulate gene expression in response to their immediate environment." The directive gene created in the 1920s has been transformed into a post-genomic, dynamic, and reactive genome (2014: 2425). It is no longer tenable to assert, as E.O. Wilson did, that "genes hold culture on a leash" (1978: 167), and to some researchers, the demoted genome has become much more interesting.

Dark matter

When scientists found that large segments of the genome were not functional, they labeled this matter disparagingly as "junk" and set it to one side. In the intervening fifteen years it has become clear that approximately 1.2% of isolated DNA segments code for proteins, and this may be an over-estimate. A 2003 article by Wayt Gibbs in *Scientific American* stated:

> [N]ew evidence...contradicts conventional notions that genes...are the sole mainspring of heredity and the complete blueprint for all life. Much as dark matter influences the fate of galaxies, dark parts of the genome exert control over the development and the distinctive traits of all organisms, from bacteria to humans.... [S]ome scientists now suspect that much of what

makes one person, and one species, different from the next are variations in the gems hidden within our "junk" DNA. (2003: 48)

The genome is home to many more actors than protein-coding genes. It is now well established that the activities of non-coding RNA (ncRNA) comprise the most comprehensive regulatory systems in complex organisms. These activities function to create the "architecture" of organisms, without which chaos would reign. To this end, ncRNA profoundly affects the timing of processes that occur during development, including stem cell maintenance, cell proliferation, apoptosis (programmed cell death), the occurrence of cancer, and other complex ailments. It has been shown recently that the epigenetic regulation of chromatin structure is of crucial importance in these processes (see chapter 5).

Numerous molecular geneticists no longer map genomes, but seek to unravel the mechanisms of cell and organ functioning that bring about evolutionary change and individual growth and development. Central to this endeavor is the understanding of gene regulation – above all how, and under what circumstances, genes are expressed and modulated. In this rapidly proliferating knowledge base, often glossed as epigenetics, organized complexity is recognized, and cells, rather than DNA segments, are the primary targets of investigation. Effects of evolutionary, historical, and environmental variables on cellular activity, developmental processes, health, and disease are incorporated into this research endeavor, much of it devoted to research into ncRNA. This emerging knowledge makes clear that the task of the genome is to respond to environments that we are currently altering at a phenomenal rate. The central dogma on which molecular genetics was founded has been exploded. Metaphors associated with the mapping of the human genome – the Book of Life, the Code of Codes, the Holy Grail – are thoroughly outmoded.

Genes as composite objects

Since the time of Mendel, when particulate inheritance began to be conceptualized as a hypothetical material entity, the gene, as it became known, has repeatedly been re-conceptualized on the basis of technological innovation, and also in part owing to its use in experimental undertakings. When Thomas Hunt Morgan delivered his Nobel lecture in 1933, he noted that there was no consensus among geneticists as to what genes were. Nevertheless, clearly *something* must account for the successes taking place with controlled breeding experiments. The hypothetical Mendelian gene was good to think with, and was made use of in experiments for two purposes: to better establish what exactly a gene might be and, at the same time, as an effective tool that allowed scientists and farmers to practice biology, notably husbandry. The concept of Mendelian genes continues to be made use of today in clinical genetics and by evolutionary biologists and population geneticists. Such genes are tools used in the detection of mutations that contribute to various diseases, or to account for environmental adaptations. But, as we have seen, from the 1950s on, the dominant way of conceptualizing genes became that of one-dimensional molecular entities; strips of determinate information.

Paradoxically, the more that genes were investigated and the genome conceptualized as a template with a well-defined molecular structure, the more difficult it became to interpret the findings that were discovered. It was evident that the usual alleles (variants) of a gene result from a large number of DNA sequences, and mutants arise in numerous ways. Thousands of DNA sequences are often involved in these activities. Because a coding gene is not a continuous sequence of DNA, but is usually composed of separate pieces of DNA that lie relatively near to each other and together code for a protein, it is argued that genes should be conceptualized as "complex, spatially discontinuous objects" (Barnes and Dupré 2008: 52), if indeed they can be thought of as material objects at all.

If genes are objects, then they must be understood as composite rather than as unitary, somewhat analogous to "the solar system, or a forest, or a cell culture" (Barnes and Dupré 2008: 53):

> If DNA is the material substrate of objects we refer to as genes, then these objects are very strange ones.... [A]n entire set of genes cannot be thought of as so many separate pieces of DNA each of which is the material substrate of one of the genes.... [T]he set of genes in a genome is not to be compared with a bag of marbles. Take a marble from the bag and the rest will remain, but take a gene from the set and other genes could well prove to be missing as well. The DNA that by virtue of what it does is part of the gene for protein X may, by virtue of something else it does, also be part of the gene for protein Y. This makes gene talk awkward and untidy in comparison with talk of the related DNA, which is ... the more accessible "theoretical entity." For this and other reasons the existence of genes may now be thought of as questionable in ways that the existence of DNA is not. (Barnes and Dupré 2008: 55)

Understanding genes as singular entities is clearly questionable, but specific protein coding sequences are indeed material in kind. Even so, on its own, DNA cannot be the origin of life, a determining force of evolution, individual development, or human health and illness, despite the continuing robust support of this position by many geneticists. Evelyn Fox Keller has described the twentieth century as the century of the gene: "The image of genes as clear and distinct causal agents, constituting the basis of all aspects of organismic life, has become so deeply embedded in both popular and scientific thought that it will take far more than good intentions, diligence, or conceptual critique to dislodge it" (2000: 136). The following chapter, in which we enter the world of epigenetics, makes clear why the genome is not the organism. A major perceptual shift is underway; one in which the gene has been demoted and nature/nurture is conceptualized as an *indivisible* entity, albeit malleable, in which nurture is the active, initiating force, to which the genome reacts.

THREE

Reinstating Nurture: From Opposition to Commingling

From its inception, eugenics, purportedly grounded in the science of genetics, was attacked by a considerable number of scientists and public figures. Tests used to distinguish the mentally fit from the unfit were condemned as unscientific, and even Galton admitted that his hunches about racial difference failed to stand up to empirical evidence. Eugenics also provided a platform for broader nature/nurture debates. Among the most articulate of critics was Lancelot Hogben, a zoologist and statistician, who granted that the application of statistical methods to study human variation was a significant advance, but noted: "Genetical science has outgrown the false antithesis between heredity and environment productive of so much futile controversy in the past" (1932: 201). Hogben insisted that variation in a population could be accounted for only by examining both "hereditary variation" and "environmental variation," and, significantly, by considering what takes place when a *specific* hereditary constitution and a *particular* kind of environment are in play. He argued strongly for recognition of the interdependence of nature and nurture.

During the mid-twentieth century, other statisticians adopted the position taken by Hogben, although debate persisted as how research should best proceed. The most divisive arguments were between followers of Hogben and those who emulated Ronald Fisher, founder of the Eugenic Society at Cambridge University and also the discipline of population genetics. Fisher attempted to account for the respective statistical contributions made separately by nature and nurture to variation evident in defined populations. Unlike Fisher's followers, the Hogben group focused on *individual* development and the variation resultant from combinations of nature and nurture to which individuals are uniquely exposed.

Arguments continued along these lines over the decades, culminating in the infamous IQ debate in the 1970s. The biologist Richard Lewontin set himself up in opposition to Arthur Jensen, who claimed that IQ is highly hereditable and that measureable differences in IQ exist among "races." Jensen and Lewontin conceptualized and judged evidence for the interaction of nature and nurture in different ways, essentially talking past each other. Like Fisher years earlier, Jensen and his colleagues partitioned variation within populations into percentages of nature and nurture and assumed that the extent of interaction between nature and nurture was small, and hence could be set to one side. In contrast, the position taken by Lewontin and colleagues was that causal mechanisms of development and resultant variation are the product of highly significant gene/environment interactions, and should be thoroughly researched to tease out the specifics. Organism and environment literally define each other and body boundaries are permeable, they argued, in a somewhat similar vein to that taken by the humoral traditions, explored in chapter 1. Lewontin, in support of Hogben's line of reasoning, argued vociferously that environment cannot be independent of the organism: "[J]ust as the information needed to specify an organism is not contained entirely in its genes, but also in its environment, so the environmental problems of the organism are a consequence of its genes" (1995: 132).

From epigenesis to epigenetics

Richard Lewontin and other like-minded biologists expressly acknowledge Conrad Hal Waddington as a great influence on their thinking. Born in 1905, Waddington came to be regarded by some as a revolutionary thinker, mostly after his death seventy years later. The

Encyclopaedia Britannica describes him as an embryologist, geneticist, and philosopher of science. He acquainted himself with paleontology while teaching at Cambridge University, and eventually became known as the founder of systems biology. Waddington explicitly derived the term "epigenetics" from the Aristotelian word "epigenesis":

> Some centuries ago, biologists held what are called "preformationist" theories of development. They believed that all the characters of the adult were present in the newly fertilized egg but packed into such a small space that they could not be properly distinguished with the instruments then available. If we merely consider each gene as a determinant for some definite character in the adult (as when we speak loosely of the "gene for blue eyes, or for fair hair"), then the modern theory may appear to be merely a new-fangled version of the old idea. But...the embryologists... have reached quite a different picture...the theory known as epigenesis, which claims that the characters of the adult do not exist already in the newly fertilized germ, but on the contrary arise gradually through a series of causal interactions between the comparatively simple elements of which the egg is initially composed. There can be no doubt...that this epigenetic point of view is correct. (Waddington 1957: 156)

Waddington initially argued that the field of epigenetics be confined to demonstrating causal interactions between genes and their products that result in the phenotype (physical traits). His position was influenced by the dawning realization of several researchers that embryological development must involve networks of interactions among genes that form a complex integrated system, and that the completely bifurcated subjects of genetics and embryology should be better integrated, although many embryologists feared that their field would be overtaken by genetics if such a move occurred. Waddington was trained in both fields; he had worked in Germany with the Nobel laureate embryologist Hans Spemann, and with the geneticist Thomas Hunt Morgan in California, and made "development" central to his arguments expressly because of its double meaning: the growth of individuals *and* evolutionary change.

Waddington's image of the "epigenetic landscape" (Figure 1) has achieved iconic status as a metaphor that is made use of today in both the arts and sciences (Baedke 2013). The path followed by the ball, canalized by the contours of the terrain through which it passes, depicts the developmental history of a particular part of the egg.

Waddington's intention when creating the epigenetic landscape was to depict a process that is anchored, but

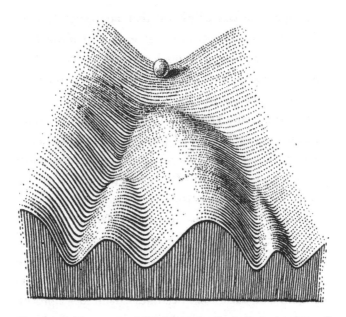

Figure 1. The original Waddington "epigenetic landscape" (Waddington 1957). (Reproduced by permission of Taylor & Francis Books UK.)

not determined, by genes that "buffer" the effects of environmental stimuli, a process implicated in both individual development and natural selection. He argued that genes are responsible only for guiding "the mechanics of development," and phenotypes result from interactions among cellular environments and genotypes. He was emphatic that no straightforward relationship exists between a gene and its phenotypic effects – any given gene does not necessarily result in the same phenotype or phenotypes; furthermore, synchronic processes in the intra-cellular environment and among genes greatly modify linear unidirectional accounts of developmental processes and evolutionary change. These arguments are today subsumed under the much-used concept of "phenotypic plasticity": the ability of an organism to create the phenotype most advantageous in response to environmental changes.

Waddington's experiments with *drosophilia* (fruit flies) showed that an adaptive response to environmental stimuli depends on a "genetically controlled reactivity" in the organism that becomes canalized – a process he termed "genetic assimilation." He recognized that what are known today as embryonic "pluripotent stem cells" become differentiated during development so that they acquire specific functions as, for example, liver or brain cells in the various tissues and organs of the body. Furthermore, he recognized "critical periods" during individual development, universally accepted today. Waddington upended the dominant thinking of his time – that genes are the source of life and determine development – when he insisted that genes must be activated and deactivated by complex intra-cellular processes. His theorizing influenced debates within both embryology and evolution, but he was aware that the image of the epigenetic landscape had limitations. Although politically active, Waddington did not find it necessary to include variables external to the body in his canalized landscape, perhaps because his research was largely confined to fruit flies.

Working in the same era as Waddington, the physician philosopher Georges Canguilhem, who was active in the French Resistance, argued for the recognition of "milieu" as a concept. Emphasizing the biological relationship between "the living and its milieu," Canguilhem insisted that the "individuality of the living does not stop at its ectodermic borders any more than it begins at the cell" (2008 [1965]: 111). The research and writing of both Canguilhem and Lewontin is at one with that of Waddington but, significantly, they extend the idea of environment *beyond the body* into the world at large. Lewontin states: "Organisms have skin, but their total environments do not. It is by no means clear how to delineate the effective environment of an organism" (2011: 23). He adds that it is important to pay attention to the ecological niche in which organisms of every kind exist as populations. For both these commentators, "nurture" is inseparable from "nature," and, at the same time, nature is enveloped by nurture.

Molecular epigenetics and the reactive genome

Waddington's work was overlooked for three decades, and several scientists claimed that it had no worth, but it was eventually revitalized to become the foundational approach of molecular epigenetics. Throughout the latter part of the twentieth century, genetic determinists had effectively ignored the concept of nurture. Epigeneticists argued, in contrast, that environments have an undeniably significant effect on cell functioning and in accounting for the phenotypes of individuals and families.

Today the majority of biologists, whatever their specialty, accept that cellular differentiation is governed by something akin to what Waddington described as the epigenetic landscape, a complex panorama of networks and feed-forward loops that determine whether or not stem cells go into a lineage. A large number also agree that environments interact directly with individual genomes, bringing about epigenetic changes. Many such changes are reversible, while others apparently are not. The biologist Scott Gilbert summarizes the position taken by researchers who continue the Waddington tradition: "Organisms have evolved [a reactive genome] to let environmental factors play major roles in phenotype determination ... the environment is instructive" (2003: 92).

One thriving subfield of particular interest to the nature/nurture debate is that of environmental epigenetics, in which researchers track the transmission of signals originating external to the body to the body interior, and vice versa. Researchers are usually careful to point out that we have yet to fully identify the mechanisms that transmit signals from social environments resulting in changes in DNA. Among several epigenetic mechanisms that control gene expression in cells, DNA methylation is receiving the most attention. Methylation is a highly conserved process found widely in both animal and plant worlds that permits any given genome to code for diversely stable phenotypes. The process, stimulated by enzyme activity, is one in which a methyl group consisting of one carbon atom bonded to three hydrogen atoms is attached to cytosine or adenine DNA nucleotides, thus blocking the transcription of genes. This permits differentiation of embryonic stem cells into specific cells and tissues. Such changes are usually permanent and unidirectional, take place *in utero* and in the early postpartum years, and continue throughout the life span.

Environmental epigeneticists posit that DNA methylation and related mechanisms have a second very important function, namely, that these processes do not take place solely as a result of endogenous stimuli, but are also responses to environmental signals *external* to the body that modulate patterns of cellular activity directly without the involvement of genes. An iconic, often-cited research project made use of a model of maternal deprivation created in rats by removing young pups from their mothers, thus curtailing maternal licking and grooming during critical developmental periods. This deprivation altered the expression of genes that regulate behavioral and endocrine responses to stress, as well as hippocampal synaptic development. These changes could be reversed if pups were returned in a matter of days to their mothers. Furthermore, when the birth mother was a poor nurturer, placement of her pups with a surrogate mother who licked and groomed them enabled the pups to flourish (Meaney et al. 1996). Crucially, it was shown that pups or foster pups left to mature with low-licking mothers not only exhibited a chronically increased stress response (in which DNA methylation and histone [spool-shaped protein] modifications were involved), but also passed this behavior on to their own pups. Hence, variation in material behavior results in biological pathways that lead to significantly different infant phenotypes that can persist into adulthood.

A substantial body of research, based largely on animal models, has now accrued supporting a position that, in addition to genes, forces internal and external to the body contribute to the phenotype of the next generation, and possibly of several generations. And work with single-celled organisms, nematodes, rodents, and primates has demonstrated transgenerational epigenetic effects. When it comes to humans, vociferous arguments take place among researchers as to whether or not such transmission occurs. The work of Marcus Pembrey and Lars Olov Bygren in Överkarlix in an isolated Swedish municipality near the Arctic Circle where, until recently, famine was frequent is portrayed in a 2005 BBC documentary, *The Ghost in Your Genes*. Based on examination of historical records of three generations of births and deaths and annual records of harvests, these researchers found strong correlations between epigenetic changes in eggs and sperm in grandparents resultant from famine, and the occurrence years later of diabetes in their children and grandchildren. They argue that these findings are proof of transgenerational epigenetic effects. Other researchers are not yet convinced.

Over the intervening decades since the time of Waddington, epigenetics has expanded into an enormous field of inquiry that includes stem cell biology, cancer biology, investigation into genome instability, and DNA repair. However, it should not be assumed that epigenetics has usurped genomics or will yet do so. The majority of researchers in genomic research ignore environment; they are concerned with genome sequencing, gene and protein functions, and the three-dimensional structure of proteins. Expectations for "precision medicine" based on whole-genome mapping and individualized drug development are very high indeed, although to date its successes have been limited. Genomic medicine furnishes, in effect, decontextualized information. In contrast, epigenetics has the potential to create dynamic, fluid images, recognized as inherently unstable, that demand contextualization in time and space.

The field has moved far beyond Waddington's original arguments. Molecular epigenetics increasingly suggests that, at the very least, we should reverse Galton's "jingle" to become nurture and nature. But Evelyn Fox Keller makes another important point: "It is a mistake to think of the development of traits as a product of causal elements interacting with one another. Indeed, the notion of interaction presupposes the existence of entities that are at least ideally separable." Nature and nurture are not in any way separable, she insists; to insert the "and" is to make them into a false dichotomy, and "development depends on the complex orchestration of multiple courses of action that involve interactions among many different kinds of elements." This "entanglement between genes and environment" results from "an immensely complex web of interactions between environmental stimuli (both internal and external to the cell) and the structure, conformation, and nucleotide sequence of the DNA molecule" (Keller 2010: 6–7). We will return to this point.

Miniaturization of the environment

Several time scales are affected by methylation processes: evolution; transgenerational inheritance; individual lifetimes; seasonal change modifications; and life-course transitions, including infancy, adolescence, menopause, and old age. The effects of these passages of time become miniaturized in the bodies of individuals and hence are researchable at the molecular level.

One of the most cited studies researching the so-called fetal "environment" reports on pregnant women affected by what is known as the Dutch Hunger Winter, the effects of which were tracked for two ensuing generations (Heijmans et al. 2008). Thirty thousand people died from starvation in the Netherlands as a result of a food embargo imposed by the Germans in World War II that brought about a complete breakdown of local food supplies, adding to the misery of an already harsh winter. Birth records collected since that time have shown that children born of women who were pregnant during the famine not only had low birth-weights, but also exhibited a disproportionally high range of developmental and adult disorders later in life including diabetes, coronary heart disease, breast and other cancers. Furthermore, it has been shown that the second generation, even though prosperous and well nourished themselves, produced low birth-weight children, who inherited similar health problems, thought to be founded on epigenetic effects. Moreover, exposure to severe food deprivation during the first trimester of pregnancy showed a substantial increase in hospitalized schizophrenia for women once adult, but not for men. The Dutch Hunger study is often cited as an example of intergenerational transmission of epigenetic effects, but doubters persist in the research world.

In addition to the effects of malnutrition on fetal development, a large literature has accrued since the 1990s showing a strong relationship between "childhood maltreatment" and negative mental health outcomes, ranging from aggressive and violent behavior to suicide. Investigations are beginning to expose the pathways of implicated epigenetic processes regarded as crucial mediators of the biological embedding of childhood maltreatment. The conclusion drawn from this research is that the "epigenome is responsive to developmental, physiological and environmental cues" (Lutz and Turecki 2014).

In 2011, epigeneticist Moshe Szyf titled a presentation he gave at a Montreal gathering "DNA Methylation: A Molecular Link between Nurture and Nature." At the time this talk was given, evidence for this link accrued primarily from animal research and from one small human study of abused adolescents who had committed suicide. Szyf insists that he is not a biological reductionist, but his presentation to an audience composed largely of molecular biologists made it easy for them to walk away with the idea that demonstration of the specifics of molecular pathways is sufficient to settle the nature/nurture puzzle once and for all. He did not venture into the social and political aspects of child abuse, present data about the histories of researched families, include narrative accounts from family members, recount what is known of the lives of the individuals who had committed suicide, or elaborate on the lives of the individuals in control groups.

Inevitably, researching human molestation is fraught with difficulties owing to ethical issues, and abuse is not amenable to measurement. But, over the years, research has become more sophisticated. Rats and humans share a similar stress mechanism and, in order to measure the effect of epigenetics on the human brain, researchers targeted the NR3C1 gene, which had previously been studied in rats. One experiment used thirty-six autopsied brains, of which twelve came from individuals who had died by suicide and had experienced childhood abuse; twelve came from suiciders who had not been subject to abuse; and another twelve were those of "normal" controls (McGowan et al. 2009). The results showed that abuse resulted in DNA methylation patterns that, in turn, altered the functioning of the NR3C1 gene such that the glands that secrete stress hormones stayed constantly alert in abused individuals, making them susceptible to anxiety, depression, and possibly suicide.

These findings are presumed to substantiate a molecular mechanism whereby nature and nurture meld as one. In this particular case, childhood adversity is associated with sustained modifications in DNA methylation across the genome, among which are epigenetic alterations in hippocampal neurons that may well interfere with processes of neuroplasticity, that is, the ability to use multiple potential pathways in the brain. The researchers acknowledge that the sample is small, and that such research cannot be thoroughly validated. The absence of a control group that experienced early life abuse and did not die by suicide is another shortcoming. Furthermore, the abuse that the subjects experienced was informally reported as exceptionally severe.

Researchers are working on drug development designed to reverse epigenetic modifications such as those described above. Making environmental changes is also certainly effective in this regard, as has clearly been observed in rats. It has recently been established that behaviorally induced methylation changes are not limited to brain tissue alone, and that changes can be detected in white blood T-cells that correlate with the brain tissue changes. This is good news for researchers, who can now use blood samples procured from living subjects, rather than be confined to donated brains.

Research findings such as those set out above have incited what has been described as an "explosion" of interest in epigenetic mechanisms of gene regulation in the brain. But we may be entering another era of somatic determinism, this time with attention directed at the cell, rather than the gene, as the focus of primary attention. Even though "environment" is conceptualized as both external and internal to the body, boundaries are often drawn by researchers so that only mother/infant dyads, or the imbibing of food, alcohol, and so on, count as significant. Reducing and containing what counts as environment is essential in order to effectively design, control, and replicate experiments. Distal aspects of environment can only be researched, almost without exception, by demonstrating statistical correlations, whereas miniaturizing the environment and confining it to proximal events reveals the precise mechanistic process of molecular changes.

The contribution of environment writ large to human development, health, and illness is rarely denied by epigeneticists. But there is a danger that miniaturization, while it reveals what takes place internal to bodies, ignores the way in which historical, social, economic, and political variables that impinge on human experience and behavior contribute both indirectly and directly to epigenetic marks. One dramatic example of misreporting of epigenetic findings about abuse and violence is an article insinuating that we know now that the "roots of violence" lie in our bodies (Johnson 2014). Environmental epigenetic findings are clearly vulnerable to abuse in the hands of individuals predisposed to painting human behavior as biologically determined.

Embedded bodies

Several years ago, the Berlin-based anthropologist Jörg Niewöhner carried out research in the Montreal laboratory headed up by Moshe Szyf. Niewöhner argues that environmental epigenetic interactions such as those researched by Szyf's group highlight the importance of thinking across different temporal horizons and spatial scales. He notes: "In epigenetic research, interpretations of findings often combine evolutionary time, trans-generational or biographic time and the 'real' time of cellular activity in order to construct a plausible argument." Environmental epigenetics of this kind produces an "embedded body" (Niewöhner 2011: 285) "heavily impregnated by its own past and by the social and material environment within which it dwells. It is a body that is imprinted by evolutionary and trans-generational time, by 'early-life,' and a body that is highly susceptible to changes in its social and material environment" (2011: 289–90). However, in the lab, a "pragmatic reductionism" prevails in which events of significance in people's lives are documented, thematically standardized, and then examined for associations with epigenetic changes. Niewöhner concludes that aspects of the social world are situated in a "quasi-natural experimental system" in this kind of research. The environment – nurture – is scientifically ordered to "fit" with the goals of molecularized epigenetics. In other words, subjective knowledge and meanings attributed to events in everyday life together with the environment writ large are set to one side, as the following examples illustrate.

Epigenetics and the womb

A field known as the "developmental origins of health and disease" (DOHaD), in which research is focused on the "fetal environment," has been in existence for several decades. Its interests have now turned to epigenetics. Prenatal exposure to "maternal stress, anxiety and depression" has repeatedly been associated with lasting effects on infant development, culminating in psychopathology later in life. A review of nearly 200 articles based on animal and a small quantity of human research concludes: "[T]he *in utero* environment is regulated by placental function and there is emerging evidence that the placenta is highly susceptible to maternal distress and is a target of epigenetic dysregulation" (Monk et al. 2012: 1361), added to which a large body of research suggests that postnatal maternal care can induce further disruptions.

Such findings are based primarily on correlations, although researchers are beginning to map segments of pathways whereby environmentally induced epigenetic marks are associated directly with behavioral outcomes pre- and postnatally. Antenatal depression and anxiety are picked out for particular attention as indicators of an *in utero* environment bringing about dysregulation. In other words, the environment is effectively scaled down to molecular activity inside a single organ of the body – the uterus and its fetal contents. Maternal bodies have become "epigenetic vectors," in Sarah Richardson's words – the symbols favored by DOHaD researchers at meetings and in books are "fetuses encapsulated in headless, legless maternal abdomens" (2015: 223). Certain researchers regard the mother's body as a genetically programmed, evolutionarily adapted system that transmits signals from past and present environments to the fetus by means of epigenetic mechanisms. As one researcher put it, epigenetic mechanisms are like "volume controls for genes" (cited in Richardson 2015: 225). This decontextualized image is not wildly inaccurate, but one hopes that clinicians are not taking it too literally.

As epigenetic changes *in utero* become increasingly implicated in medical conditions, ranging from autism to diabetes, the womb and its environments will be monitored ever more closely. A warning sent out to its members by the American Academy of Pediatrics in 2011 cautioned about the harm caused to children by "toxic stress" that will result in damaged "biological memories." Ilina Singh notes that emphasis has previously been given to improving environmental variables assumed to affect the wellbeing of children, the Head Start Program of the 1960s being one that proved, ultimately, to have few positive results. Epigenetic findings now justify making interventions as early as possible, preferably before infants are born (Singh 2012). This will entail close monitoring of families, primarily pregnant women and young mothers, whose behavior will be subjected to surveillance designed to avoid fetal and infant stress that raises the specter of unproductive youth who will be a drain on the economy.

Accumulating evidence has shown that diet, smoking, and excess alcohol consumption in pregnant mothers negatively affect the fetus, at times with serious consequences. Medical and social support for childbearing women is to be lauded but, as Singh states, the possibility is that revamped home visits to pregnant women, such as those being carried out through a partnership of nurses and family practitioners in New York, might well become, in effect, "womb visits." The poverty and often violent living conditions of many women are liable to be ignored, and attention is likely to focus almost exclusively on the pregnant belly and its contents (Singh 2012). Experiments with mice suggest that traumatic experiences can leave epigenetic marks in semen (Hughes 2014), but "sperm visits" are not, as yet, taking place, it seems.

Obviously, fetal malaise and that experienced by young children are at times caused directly by parental and step-parental behavior. The situation is frequently aggravated by the socioeconomic status of the family and may be exacerbated by substance abuse. However, history, politics, poverty, social isolation, racism, chronic discrimination, war, and other major social disruptions should be given consideration equal to or greater than that of everyday family life when attempting to account for apparent fetal distress.

Food as environment

Nutritional epigenetics is a field attracting a great deal of attention because it is hoped that it will throw light on the so-called "obesity epidemic" currently affecting many countries, affluent or otherwise. Hannah Landecker argues that researchers conceptualize food as an "epigenetic" factor that functions in the regulation of gene expression, in turn, linked to several medical conditions, including cancer, metabolic syndrome, obesity, and diabetes. In other words, food itself is a form of "environmental exposure" (Landecker 2011: 167) in which the molecularized environment is food chemistry: "[S]ocial things (food, in particular) enter the body, are digested, and in shaping metabolism, become part of the body-in-time, not by building bones and tissues, but by leaving an imprint on a dynamic bodily process," namely, the expression of genes (2011: 177). The environment is miniaturized and decontextualized in this instance from the lived experience of the many individuals who cannot afford nutritious food for themselves and their families. If the greater milieu were taken into consideration, then accounts about causation would be politicized and dramatically broadened to include inequalities, discrimination, and the peddling of junk food.

Clearly this work is of singular importance, but the majority of researchers to date miniaturize "nurture," and entities and events assumed to be *directly* responsible for intra-cellular epigenetic effects are singled out: pregnant women, infant care, abusive families, lack of adequate nutrition, and toxic exposures inside the household. Focusing exclusively on these proximate variables, scientifically valuable though they are, has grave limitations, because historical and sociopolitical contexts that incite violence, poverty, deprivation, inequality, stigma, and racism remain unaddressed. Consider, for example, research on the disproportionate burden of abnormalities, disease, and mortality born by

African Americans in the United States in connection with low birth-weight (Kreiger and Rowley 1992) and cardiovascular disease (Kuzawa and Sweet 2009); or the phenomenon known as "the Glasgow Effect," used to describe dramatic class differences in that city (known as Europe's sickest) in terms of disease incidence and life expectancy, in which epigenetics has been implicated (Ash 2014).

Social deprivation

Research carried out with Romanian children living in orphanages at the start of the twenty-first century makes clear that a paucity of social relations can bring about significant life-long harm that may well have intergenerational effects. A randomized clinical trial was conducted in which over sixty orphans aged 8 and 9 were moved into good foster care homes, at the expense of the involved researchers from the United States, while a control group of similar size was left to languish in the orphanage. The study demonstrated, not surprisingly, that foster care was much more effective for the wellbeing and development, mental and physical, of these children than was the orphanage setting, in which a single adult may be responsible for twelve to fifteen charges. Of particular interest was that, as compared with never-institutionalized children, the orphaned children exhibited less development in both the gray and white matter in their brains. Foster placement quickly improved development of white matter, although gray matter did not recover. Furthermore, the majority of institutionalized children showed shorter telomere lengths (the segment of DNA that occurs at the end of each chromosome). Elizabeth Blackburn, who has worked her whole life on this subject, argues that shortened telomeres "powerfully quantify life's insults" (Blackburn and Epel 2012: 170). These findings were communicated to the Romanian government, in the hope, one assumes, that increased efforts will be made to foster the many children still living in orphanages as a result of the Ceauçescu regime. Attempts to map the epigenetic pathways of these findings, and those obtained from other orphanages, are now underway, with some success. Tracking links between brain development and successful fosterage exposes the damage likely done to the millions of abandoned, dispossessed, and refugee children who are left to languish in institutions, or moved repeatedly from one foster care setting to another. The Romanian case well illustrates how epigenetic findings can be used to support demands for social and political change in connection with vulnerable populations.

Aging and epigenetics

When DNA methylation was examined across twelve genome loci considered susceptible to Alzheimer's disease (AD), it was found that "age-specific epigenetic drift" from a previously established norm was apparent in brain tissue taken from individuals who had been diagnosed with AD prior to death, as compared to normal controls. Epigenetic effects accumulate throughout life from conception on. Deviations between epigenetic age and chronological age increase in later life, but it is not known what causes this drift, and inter-individual variability is evident. Brain tissue obtained from identical twins, for example, had markedly different levels of DNA methylation. One twin had been diagnosed with AD at aged 60 and died sixteen years after the diagnosis, and the other died aged 79, with no signs of dementia. The twin who was demented had significantly lower DNA methylation in his brain tissue than did his brother, and had been exposed extensively to high pesticide levels in connection with his earlier employment, a factor considered to be highly significant. Correlation links between exposure to lead in early life, epigenetic drift, and AD have also been demonstrated.

It has long been known that no one gene causes late-onset AD, and that clusters of genes may put individuals at risk under conditions that are poorly understood. It is also well established that diet, exercise, and an active social life constitute a protective environment, whereas poverty and social isolation increase risk. These findings, and many others from epidemiology and neuro-imaging, challenge the dominant approach taken by the medical world to Alzheimer's, namely, that this phenomenon is a burgeoning epidemic of a readily diagnosable disease for which a silver bullet can be found. Epigenetic findings strongly suggest that neuro-protection is as important as is the elusive search for a cure for AD (Lock 2013) and, furthermore, indicate that the reductionist interventions characteristic of bio-medicine, in which by far the majority of attention is directed at curing the body – at nature, alone – are not only inadequate, but also way too late.

From causality to contingency

The above illustrations are of epigenetic findings deduced primarily from basic science research, in which the experiences of infants *in utero*, treatment of young children, nutrition, and aging processes are associated with DNA methylation, by correlation or causally, often with negative outcomes. It is also known that epigenetic mechanisms influence the expression of immune system-related genes, thus modifying the development of innate and adaptive immune responses to a whole range of conditions. These findings are of exceptional interest and point the way to further research with great potential for solidifying what has recently come to light. However, the tendency of laboratory researchers is to nod at environment writ large, that is, at social, economic, and political variables that so often incite epigenetic changes, but then to set them to one side. It is fair to state, as does Moshe Szyf, that epigenetics has shown a link between nurture and nature, but we do not know the constellation of events that precedes the proximate causes of DNA methylation. Nor do we know why a good number of individuals of all ages exhibit a resilience that enables them to cope effectively with trauma of various kinds and degrees. We assume such people do not have methylation changes, but this may not be the case – we simply do not know, although resilience is unlikely following massive exposure to chemical toxins.

The history of genetics shows that struggles over what will count as authoritative knowledge have been the norm for over 100 years. The form of these disputes was established with the introduction at the beginning of the twentieth century of the genotype/phenotype distinction. This distinction caused friction among the separate fields of heredity, embryology, and developmental biology, each of which brought a particular orientation to research in connection with the transmission of heritable material from one generation to another. Waddington, whose work transcended disciplinary interests, made a significant response in the mid-twentieth century by positing an epigenetic landscape. Another, more recent approach is that of "developmental systems theory," advanced by the philosophers of science Susan Oyama and colleagues, in which they argue that researchers must "investigate how a trait actually develops, what resources its reliable development depends upon, whether there are many developmental routes to this outcome, or only one, over what range of parameters is this developmental outcome stable, and how the 'environment' changes as a function of initial development differences that produce this trait" (Griffiths 2001: 4). This restless universe is contingent at every turn; it is one in which environments – nurture – bring about changes in genome expression, the origins of which cannot be discerned by investigating disassembled units in laboratories. Space does not permit a discussion of the changes taking place in the world of evolutionary biology, but Eva Jablonka and Marion Lamb (2014) provide a remarkable overview of what they describe as a "new synthesis" grounded in epigenetic findings.

From versus to symbiosis: the microbiome and the metagenome

Emerging knowledge about the world of microbiomes opens another remarkable window into the permeability of human bodies and nature/nurture relationships, and further problematizes any simplistic understanding of the human genome as equivalent to the human being. In addition to the human genome, genomes of other organisms, including bacteria, viruses, and fungi, are present in the human body. The majority of these residents live in the human intestine, where adults harbor a teeming number of microbes, but they are also present in the mouth, scalp, on the skin, and in all the crevices and orifices of the body. Research has shown that endogenous retroviruses, and, indirectly, bacteria, via the gut–brain axis, are probably involved in brain development. The microbiome, the total of the symbiotic bacteria that work on our behalf, but equally to their own benefit, has approximately 3 million genes, exceeding the number of human genes by a factor of 150:1. The Human Microbiome Project, a National

Institutes of Health feasibility study, has been underway for eight years, and has revealed that each human microbiome is unique, like fingerprints. It is not possible, therefore, to assemble a Human Microbiome to be inserted into the HGP, as was the hope.

Given that the microbial ecosystem plays an indispensable role in the functioning of individuals' immune system, and hence contributes to discrimination between self and non-self, and, further, produces certain beneficial compounds that we cannot make for ourselves, we are not merely host to our microbiomes – these symbionts are integral to "us." The resultant human "metagenome" is composed of well over 98% microbial genes including those found in the human genome. A tightly bounded, autonomous, human simply does not exist.

A fetus may be exposed to bacteria in its mother's womb that ultimately can be beneficial to it. It is also exposed as it passes through the birth canal, becoming further coated with some of its mother's microbial cells, which begin to multiply rapidly. It has been shown that infants born by Cesarean section, which is on the increase worldwide, are at higher risk for allergies and asthma as they mature. Breast-feeding, handling by the family, contact with pets, bed linen, and so on, add to the microbial load, so that the human body by late infancy has become a microbially packed ecosystem. Every microbiome is different; even identical twins do not share the same microbial inhabitants. The microbiome, weighing in at about a kilogram, is perhaps best thought of as a human organ system, one in which communication takes place across the entire microbial system. The human genome *alone* is not the fount of human life and wellbeing, and without our symbiotic companions we could not survive. Numerous genomes are implicated in each human life, but no one of these determines who we are and what we become. Our permeable skin-bound selves comprise a collection of ecosystems, of miniaturized communities that are products of our evolutionary past, more recent historical events, and social and political contingencies of many kinds. We are merely part of a complex assemblage. This emerging knowledge transforms the nature/nurture debate entirely – these entities are no longer confined to what humans are, or to what they do, because we are more microbe than human.

We are poised to relegate genetic determinism in which "nature" holds all the cards, and are entering an epoch when environments in their many guises are being positioned once again as vital, active participants in life itself, whether by acting directly on our genes, our microbiomes, or indirectly, via diet, behaviors, and exposures to specific environments. Microbiomes are not haphazard, and the bacteria that compose the human microbiome represent numerous phyla, each of which has a different repertoire of capabilities. But their daily activities vary according to the microenvironments in which they exist. The microbiome is exquisitely sensitive, and can change in ratio and proportion – within two or three days – in response to dietary changes relating to food availability. Part of this shift involves changes in the genes that the microbiome expresses that can be beneficial to the body. The human genome is not a passive bystander to these activities, and contributes to the composition of the microbiome of persons, thus influencing individual phenotypes, including proclivities for certain illnesses. This complex ecosystem is meticulously tuned to adapt continuously to the vagaries of human life.

It is clear that the microbial mix at work today in North America and Europe deals primarily with the digestion of sugars, fats, and proteins, whereas the microbiomes of people living in Africa and South America have been shown to be more diverse and manage plant fiber particularly effectively. Hence, children living in countries such as Malawi and Bangladesh, and the Yanomami in Venezuela, Hadza in Tanzania, and Matsés in Peru, have microbes in their digestive tracts that "fit" with their local diets and environments. It is possible that our early ancestors harbored even greater variety in their microbiomes. The microbiome of Hadza exhibits remarkable taxonomic diversity, making it possible for them to deal with a constantly changing seasonally dependent food supply, as well as the presence of numerous parasites and bacteria that frequently invade their bodies. The microbiomes of Hadza women and men are not the same because their respective diets are different: a woman's diet has many more tubers in it than that of a man, and it also assists in supplying sufficient nutrients during pregnancy, increasing the chances of reproductive success. To date, knowledge about the microbiome has been based largely on animal modeling, but as findings increasingly accumulate using human subjects, the remarkable, indispensable contribution made by healthy, diverse microbiomes to their human partners is becoming glaringly apparent.

Ridding our bodies of bacteria has been a major goal of modern healthcare systems; the development of antibiotics is regarded as one of the greatest innovations of the twentieth century, and millions of lives have been saved as a result. But perhaps the enormous efforts we make to stay clean in daily life amount to a "germophobia." By the age of 18, the average American child has received from ten to twenty courses of antibiotics, most of which have resolved a potentially serious infection. It is becoming clear that a price must be paid for ridding bacteria from our ecosystem.

At the beginning of the twentieth century, *H. pylori* was present in the stomach of just about everyone worldwide. This bacterium has been associated with ulcers and at times to the onset of stomach cancer, and great efforts were made to wipe it out. It is now evident that *H. pylori* also performs beneficial functions that start in infancy – although in certain people in adult life it can cause damage, normally it is symbiotic and protects its human "partner." Individuals who do not have *H. pylori* in their stomachs are far more likely to have had asthma as children than those whose guts harbor the bacterium, and an absence of *H. pylori* is associated with increased risk for obesity and hence Type 2 diabetes, because this bacteria is linked to two hormones that regulate the appetite. Coupled with the high intake of sugar and fat in the diets of so many people, and a sedentary lifestyle, the absence of *H. pylori* is clearly troubling. What is more, antibiotics are administered in very high doses to the poultry and meat that we consume in order that they put on weight quickly, and are then slaughtered at a younger age, thus increasing profits. Antibiotic residues are often passed along to humans, adding to our vulnerability.

Accumulating knowledge about the microbiome forces us to rethink ourselves from inside out and outside in, demanding a radical transformation in our ideas about the relationship of nature/nurture. This shift makes strikingly evident localized diversity among human bodies, individually and in groups, based on environmental contexts to which the microbial contribution, both exterior and interior to the body, is immense. Recent findings about Neanderthal and Denisovan genes in the human genome expose yet further diversity, in this case a genetic admixture of very long duration. When *Homo sapiens* ranged outside Africa into what is now Europe and Asia, they encountered populations of Neanderthals and Denisovans until about 40,000 years ago with sufficient frequency that the DNA of many modern humans comprises between 1.5% and 2% Neanderthal DNA and between 3% and 5% of Denisovan DNA. Individuals whose ancestors never left Africa have no such DNA. The ceaseless movement of humans, usually in search of security and food, keeps our reactive human genome and metagenome busy. Nature/nurture have been inseparably commingled in humans from eons past to the present moment.

FOUR

Accruing Biosocial Momentum

Dualistic theoretical approaches to the human body have posited, on the one hand, a *biological* body refashioned through the long-term evolution and adaptation of species and populations and, on the other hand, a *social* body exposed to the exigencies of history, culture, politics, economics, and community life. Epigenetics, as we have seen, potentially challenges this dualism by demonstrating at the molecular level a fusion of the material and social. This challenge not only reverberates in the worlds of biology and medicine but also has implications for other disciplines that embraced a dualistic approach to the body during the last century.

The Superorganic and its critics

Throughout the twentieth century, the majority of social scientists assumed that for research purposes the material body should be "bracketed," set to one side, and left in the hands of biologists. The highly influential anthropologist Alfred Kroeber, first cousin of Hermann J. Muller, found justification for creating this marked dichotomy between nature and nurture by drawing on the work of Weismann. Kroeber insisted that Weismann had proved beyond doubt that the Lamarckian structure was hollow. He was especially struck by Weismann's argument that a wall exists between "gamete and zygote" (the unfertilized sex cell and the fertilized cell), and he inferred from this that biology cannot in any way explain the achievements of human society. Kroeber chastised sociologists, historians, anthropologists, and other theorists for having "imitated" biologists, and insisted that in order to account for social phenomena it is necessary to "disregard the organic as such and to deal only with the social" (Kroeber 1917: 184).

Kroeber's essay "The Superorganic," published in 1917, became the canonical argument explaining why biology has no place in cultural anthropology. Heredity does not influence the accomplishments of a group relative to other groups, Kroeber insisted (1917: 203), and hence no connection exists between organic and social evolution. For him, the possession of values (morals) sets humans apart from animals: "The dawn of the social...is not a link in any chain, not a step in a path, but a leap to another plane" (1917:209). Even so, Kroeber agreed with Galton's theories about the inheritance of intelligence because he firmly believed that "characters of mind are subject to heredity much like traits of the body." Kroeber stressed that the Superorganic (a term he used interchangeably with history, culture, and civilization) is not *merely* a collection of individuals, because it is greater than the sum of its parts. Publication of Kroeber's work had a huge impact in the United States, placing the discipline of cultural anthropology on a secure footing.

Kroeber gave no acknowledgment to the French sociologist Émile Durkheim who had earlier taken a similar position. To this day it is not clear whether this was a genuine oversight or something darker. Durkheim wrote in 1912 that "man is double" and deliberately bifurcated a universal biological body from a "higher," morally imbued "socialized" body (1961 [1912]: 29). The position taken by Marcel Mauss, Durkheim's nephew, softened this stark dualism when he argued for recognition of interdependence among the physical body and psychosocial and social domains. Mauss's position was that the body is the "first and most natural tool of man" (1973 [1934]: 75). Anthropological research has for decades demonstrated how the body is everywhere made use of as a natural symbol. Body ornamentation, depilation, clothing, and hairstyles have symbolic meaning usually signifying social belonging, wealth, hierarchy, gendered difference, and so on. The skin, tattooed or scarified, can function as social memory – the biography of an embodied life course, both private and public, individualized but, equally, connected with others by means of touch and inscriptions.

In his early work, the French sociologist Pierre Bourdieu adopted Mauss's concept of *habitus* to argue that lifestyle, values, dispositions, and expectations of particular social groups are acquired and embodied through the activities and experiences of everyday life. In part, Bourdieu was reacting to a rigid dualism posited by Claude Lévi-Strauss between so-called "mental structures" and the world of material objects, including the body itself. Numerous publications show how the body, often as part of ritual performance, is used as an expression of self, consciously or otherwise, marking both belonging to and dissent from the social order. It is also well established that the subjective experience and verbal expression of illness are deeply informed by cultural norms. Body/mind dualisms are confronted in this research, but these theorists do not delve beneath the skin; universal interiority remains intact – an assumed given.

Michel Foucault argues that bodies become subjectively and objectively known through discursive practices. His position is that bodies are "disciplined" and collectivized by medical discourse and technologies, with the result that they are recognized, by government, medical professionals, and the public alike, as bounded biological entities subdivided according to medical specialty. His concept of biopower is an attempt to specify how governmental interests in populations, particularly with respect to birth, death, illness, and economic production, are expressed in mechanisms of surveillance. For Foucault, the language of science is made use of in the interests of governance. His arguments, while criticized as being overly derived from a European, notably French, perspective, were path-breaking, and stimulated a vast literature critical of both biopower and biomedical practices narrowly focused on nature and its pathologies.

Opening up the black box

Spurred on by Simone de Beauvoir's argument that "one is not born, but rather becomes, a woman" (1973 [1949]: 301) the question of sexual inequality came to the fore in the 1970s, and the concept of "gender"

– attributes acquired through socialization – was adopted to counter a common assumption of biology as destiny. Feminists worked to repudiate such essentialist accounts, arguing that the body is socially constructed through discourse. Numerous publications appeared in which the gendering of bodies was made evident by situating women's lives in the specific histories, politics, and economics of their time and place.

Judith Butler, sympathetic up to an extent with the construction of gender, nevertheless argued that this approach was wanting. She insists, as have others, that the concept of nature has a history, and that the "figuring of nature as a blank and lifeless page, as that which is, as it were, always already dead, is decidedly modern" (1993:3). Butler points out that a "regime of heterosexuality" operates to circumscribe the very materiality of sex, and makes clear how, in so doing, numerous bodies, including those of gays and lesbians, are de-legitimated and disqualified as natural. Butler moves beyond Foucault by proposing that we return to the idea of matter, not as a fixed site, but as "a process of materialization that stabilizes over time to produce the effect of boundary, fixity, and surface we call matter." Sex must be theorized, as must gender (1993: 10). Thus, we move towards a position in which nurture and nature, both, are constructed and bounded. Butler claims that there is no such thing as a "pure" body, but even she does not probe beneath the skin.

With the exception of biologists and clinicians, the interiority of the modern body was left intact until the late 1970s, when feminist historians and biologists together with philosophers of science in effect entered it in order to demonstrate that medical knowledge is not an unmediated "truth." They pointed out that knowledge about the body, even when grounded in the biosciences, draws on malleable concepts to explain what medical technologies make visible. Such observations are decontextualized and objectified. "Gene," as we have seen, is one such concept; so too are many named diseases, such as Alzheimer's and depression, which have multiple, complex etiologies, and resist precise taxonomic classification and treatment. Furthermore, biomedical knowledge is fragmented because the various specialties "see" and understand body parts and their functioning in different ways (Lock 2013; Mol 2002). These researchers do not dismiss the "universal" body outright (an entity that is indispensable to contemporary medical practice), but bodies are contextualized in time and space. The interdependence of history, society, politics, and technological innovations is brought to the fore, on the basis of which facts are made known that become outmoded when a shake-up or paradigm shift takes place based on newly consolidated knowledge (Kuhn 1996).

Local biologies

Everyone knows, of course, that the human body is not a universal, but the assumption in biomedicine is usually that variation is, in practice, insignificant, even though every clinician and most patients know that certain drugs work well with some people and not others. Epigenetic findings demand a radical shift in conceptualization of the human body in which variation among humans, and the reasons for its existence, take center stage. This shift, if and when it is more widely recognized in the medical world, will not overturn most current biomedical practice, but several sub-disciplines, including preventive medicine, psychiatry, and maternal and child health will be deeply affected.

Researchers in epidemiology and public health are concerned primarily with statistical correlations that reveal the unequal distribution of health, illness, and medical care and not with body interiority per se. Even so, such researchers adhere primarily to the basic assumptions of biomedicine, namely, that body interiority is in effect universal, and differences in the incidence of disease, life expectancy, infant mortality, and variations in physiology and nutritional requirements are fully accounted for by geographical location and/or social conditions. Nurture is standardized by epidemiologists as clustered variables that destabilize the normal body under specific environmental conditions. Usually these so-called "gene/environment interactions" are divided into percentage contributions to the condition of any one body, although certain epidemiologists are now working closely with epigeneticists and no longer dichotomize nature and nurture.

Biological anthropologists have shown repeatedly that genotypic and phenotypic variation exists among humans based on the environments in which communities have existed throughout human evolution. An inability to digest cow's milk without discomfort (lactose intolerance) among much of the world's population is just one example, as are hemoglobin variations that arose among human populations in response to living in environments infested with malaria-carrying mosquitoes.

Taking a different approach from that used by biological anthropologists, research in the 1980s that used statistical and ethnographic methods unexpectedly uncovered biological variation in connection with the end of menstruation. This midlife transition was investigated using non-clinical populations of middle-aged women aged between 45 and 55 inclusively, drawing on statistically comparable samples of over 1,300 subjects in Canada, nearly 8,000 in the United States, and over 1,300 in Japan. Only 19% of Japanese women reported that they had experienced a hot flash at some time in the past, and both frequency and intensity of flashes was much lower than among US and Canadian respondents, nearly 60% of whom had experienced this physiological reaction. Japanese women had little sleep disturbance, corroborating reports about relatively mild hot flashes. Occurrence of night sweats was extremely low in Japan, and not linked by women to the end of menstruation. In-depth interviews with healthcare professionals and individual women in both Japan and North America revealed that the end of menstruation is conceptualized and experienced very differently in these locations, with significant social and medical consequences (Lock 1993).

Prior to this investigation, the assumption was that informally reported differences in the experience of the end of menstruation would be explained entirely by cultural expectations about this stage of the lifecycle. However, these findings suggested that the embodied experience of physical sensations, whether of wellbeing, discomfort, illness, or disease, are informed in part by the physical body, itself contingent upon evolutionary, historical, environmental, and social variables. Among variables in this particular example is language usage. When the research was conducted, no one word existed in Japanese to describe a hot flash, although several non-specific words were used. Today, following medicalization of menopause, "*hotto furashu*" (adopted from English) is commonly used. Furthermore, popular knowledge about the experience of end of menstruation, including widely disseminated biomedical knowledge, was drawn on by women in both North America and Japan. But this knowledge and these expectations were significantly different in the two locations.

Furthermore, the incidence of breast cancer, osteoporosis, and heart disease is lower in Japan than in North America, pointing to further biological variation particularly significant at this stage of life. One of the present authors (Lock 1993) created the concept of "local biologies" to account for these findings in an effort to destabilize the universal body, and to displace the idea that symptoms supposedly characteristic of "white" populations are typical of the end of menstruation elsewhere. Recent research suggests that life-long dietary practices, notably extensive use of soy from early life, may in large part account for the Japanese experience. Similar findings have been made in China, but not with the same consistency as in Japan.

The concept of local biologies, widely used among medical anthropologists, contextualizes human bodies at the hub of processes and events external and internal to the body, not altogether dissimilar to ideas entertained by epigeneticists, although anthropologists are much more disposed than are epigeneticists to consider the contribution made by historical, economic, political, and cultural variables to the biology of individuals and populations.

The Anthropocene: nature in retreat

Pressure to recognize a newly emerging geological epoch, the "Anthropocene," successor to the last interglacial epoch, the "Holocene," is causing heated discussion. There is little doubt that we are now in an era when humans have become the dominant environmental force on earth, but when, exactly, this trend commenced is subject for debate. Geologists must peg their estimates to a so-called "golden spike" that appears as a marker in ice-cores, the ocean, lake sediments, and soils. Hence, some have selected July 16, 1945 as the key date, the day when the first atomic bomb was set off, signaling unprecedented levels of radiation. Environmentally oriented biologists and chemists concerned with climate change focus on the industrial revolution that commenced in the late 1700s, with its massive combustion, pollution, and output of carbon emissions, and other scientists insist that the long history of human activity on the environment over many centuries, even millennia, must be taken into consideration.

These changes took place at different times throughout the world and expanded greatly with colonization, giving rise to an ecological imperialism today visible virtually everywhere. Ultimately, no matter whether the Anthropocene is designated or not as a new geological epoch, the reality is that humans have been transforming the planet for centuries, and the continued expansion of fossil fuel use is speeding up this impact, among which climate change will be irreversible if change does not take place speedily. This emerging geopolitics is on a new scale, and gathering knowledge about environmental epigenetics complicates the long-standing separation made between "nature's handiwork" and the "artificial" products of human creativity – the Anthropocene signals the collapse of this distinction between natural history and human history.

The current era does not imply solely a conflation of the natural and the social, but suggests a radical change in perspective. The most striking feature of the Anthropocene is that it is the first geological epoch in which a defining force, namely, that of humans, is *conscious of its role*. In the (gendered) language of Fairfield Osborn, "It is man's earth now" (1948: 66). Nature has been pushed into retreat, and we live today with a voracious nurture.

Numerous political, environmental, and social theorists are zooming out, emphasizing the interconnected world of Gaia and the detrimental signatures of humans on the global front. In addition to direct destruction of the planetary ecosystem, a threat of vital debasement is increasingly evident in households globally – at a time of an escalating shortage of natural resources owing to climate change and endless capitalistic development, millions of families are displaced and can no longer maintain subsistence economies.

Molecularized biology, intent on revealing what is within, has resisted looking at the bigger picture, at the "biopolitics" of daily life, that is, government responsibility to ensure that citizens do not live in toxic environments or lack access to healthy food, clean air and water, and satisfactory housing. The effects of the

Anthropocene are not uniformly distributed across the planet; their impact varies based on the unequal distribution of wealth. It is possible that the UN and other organizations concerned with human rights will use epigenetic findings to promote the legalization of free access to the basic necessities of life for everyone, but it will fall on national and local government to put such practices into effect.

Toxic invasions

Growing public understanding worldwide about the impact on health of a lack of access to clean water and nutritious food fuels anxieties about the wellbeing of households and communities, many members of which are cognizant of their increasing exposure to toxic chemicals, radiation, contaminated food, and stress caused largely by industrial development, building materials, and household products.

For over a decade, researchers have been working to elucidate the effects on neurodevelopment of neurotoxin exposure *in utero* and in early life. A survey of 201 neurotoxins, ranging from arsenic to benzene and polychlorinated biphenyls (PCBs), concluded that hundreds of chemicals are damaging to the developing brains of children, although timing and exposure levels are significant. Currently more than 13 million deaths worldwide, associated with a range of disease endpoints, are linked annually to environmental pollutants. It is emphasized that these epigenetic changes are potentially reversible and hence preventive measures are feasible. Lead is the most closely researched toxin to date, and no safe level of exposure during the early years of human development is acceptable. Decreased brain volume is one effect of lead exposure, most pronounced in males. Research has also shown negative effects of lead exposure on language function.

Gerald Markowitz and David Rosner (2014) have graphically described the ongoing lead paint scandal in the United States that unfolded over the past half-century. Millions of children have been exposed in their homes to potential lead poisoning, although reliable numbers are not available. It is estimated that over 500,000 children between 1 and 5 years old have lead levels above that which policy makers currently regard as safe. Reminiscent of the infamous Tuskegee experiments that commenced in 1932 in rural Alabama, 100 children, mostly African American, some less than a year old, living in family dwellings where lead paint had been liberally applied were not relocated to clean housing, but monitored for years to determine the effects of lead exposure on their development. These research subjects have been described as "canaries in the coalmine."

Methyl mercury accumulates in fish, which, if consumed frequently, can affect fetal neurodevelopment in humans. US regulatory agencies have attempted to control exposures by issuing fish consumption advisories to women of childbearing age. Consumption of fish is particularly high among certain, usually poor, Native Americans, both urban and rural, who feel targeted for their "bad" dietary choice exposing their children to "non-normative" diets. Mothers are held directly responsible for developmental problems among their children, but one tribal representative, noting that consumption of fish is part of the cultural and spiritual lives of the Umatilla people, after commenting that he needed to live without fearing for his life or the lives of his children stated: "We need to see the EPA [Environmental Protection Agency] setting goals and standing firm to make things clean again.... Ultimately we need to clean up the fish and the river" (Mansfield 2012: 367).

In the Arctic, the effects of toxins such as dioxin and PCBs are more devastating than elsewhere. Legislation against these chemicals is not yet effective in the extreme north, yet toxic residues slowly drift towards the Arctic and accumulate there, making it one of the most contaminated places on earth. The body fat of seals, whales, and walruses hunted for food is highly contaminated, as is the breast milk of many Inuit women. A politically active Inuit grandmother is quoted as stating: "When women have to think twice about breast-feeding their babies, surely that must be a wake-up call to the world" (Johansen 2003: 479). The situation is exacerbated because the cost of store-bought food is beyond the reach of very many Arctic residents.

A recent article about a biologist working at the University of California, Berkeley (Aviv 2014), tells a disturbing story about one of the world's largest agribusinesses producing the herbicide atrazine, estimated to be worth around $300 million a year. It is reported that research findings about the toxic effects of atrazine resulted in what appears to be a systematic effort to debunk the researcher's findings. Similarly, the American chemical industry sought to quash findings about the toxicity associated with bisphenol, and the former Conservative government in Canada (2006–15) refused to legislate effectively against asbestos, although it is the top workplace killer. Efforts to rid the environment of such chemicals are fraught with dangers other than their toxicity. Julia Adeney Thomas suggests that historians and biologists "are now confronted with the problem of how the postwar proliferation of biochemicals disrupts our assumed 'universal biological substrate' across space and time"; she suggests that "sudden chemical acceleration now separates us physiologically from prewar human beings and from our more vulnerable contemporaries" (2014: 1601), although every household is vulnerable to some extent.

Understandably, there is widespread concern about the condition of the food we eat. Early in 2012, it was announced in Iceland that one of the main importers of salt was selling "industrial" salt to producers of human food. Salt sales had been deregulated, with the result that the bodies of practically every Icelander had been dosed for years with salt intended for entirely different purposes, including sanitation, oil production, the manufacture of drugs, and the de-freezing of icy roads. The issue caused a massive public outcry, and highlights intimate relations among porous, vulnerable bodies, their governance, and capitalist interests.

A milk scandal erupted in China in 2008 when it was found that milk and infant formula, together with other food materials, had been adulterated with melamine cyanurate and other toxic compounds. An estimated 300,000 victims were affected, including six infants who died from kidney damage, and another 54,000 babies who needed hospital care. The poison had been added to these milk products to make them appear as though they had high protein content. In a separate incident in China four years earlier, diluted milk resulted in thirteen infant deaths from malnutrition. These catastrophes, and others involving dietary and pet food in many parts of the world, have alerted publics to the toxic residues present in so much of what is sold for daily consumption. For many people, under increasing pressure from irresponsible government and corrupt enterprises, nature has become dangerously unnatural.

Malnutrition and the epigenome

Globally, nearly 2 million children die from malnutrition each year. Biological differences have been shown between infants who suffer from two common forms of serious protein-energy malnutrition: kwashiorkor (a protein deficiency resulting in edema) and marasmus (inadequate energy intake in all forms, including protein). This research, carried out in Jamaica, commenced in 1962 and continued for thirty years, during which time over 1,100 infants with severe acute malnutrition were admitted to University Hospital, Kingston. It was found that those infants diagnosed with kwashiorkor had considerably higher birth-weights than did infants diagnosed with marasmus. The authors concluded that mechanisms associated with physiological "plasticity" are operative *in utero* and that these children have distinctively different types of metabolism (Forrester et al. 2012: 4). Of the two conditions, children more often die from kwashiorkor, although less wasting takes place as compared to marasmus.

Researchers characterize marasus as "metabolically thrifty" and kwashiorkor as "metabolically profligate," resulting in distinctly different phenotypes. They propose that when the maternal diet is nutritionally low, causing marasmus, fetal metabolism "anticipates" *in utero* a postnatal environment of scarcity, and low birth-weights are assumed to be evidence of this process, an apparent survival strategy that kwashiorkor does not permit. The authors argue that this finding provides evidence in support of the fitness-enhancing effects in childhood of "anticipatory responses" *in utero*.

Along a different line, the same research team argues that evidence exists of "developmentally plastic processes" that contribute significantly to obesity, in addition to the role played by lifestyle and individual genotypes. No claim is made that developmental pathways in which methylation is involved cause obesity directly, but it is argued that the risk of genetically predisposed individuals for obesity in later life is increased. Based on a hypothesis known as the "mismatch pathway," it is posited that "evolved adaptive responses of a developing organism to anticipate future adverse environments" can have maladaptive consequences if the environment is other than "biologically anticipated" (Gluckman and Hanson 2008: 124). In other words, the bodies of fetuses and young infants exposed to nutritionally deprived diets may be epigenetically prepared to deal with deprivation – a situation that can cause havoc in food-rich environments. In addition, maternal diabetes, maternal obesity, and infant overfeeding are associated with increased risk of obesity in adult life.

Animal research and a small number of studies on humans suggest that evolution equips organisms with the ability to respond relatively quickly to novel environments, and that such responses may be transmitted to the next generation, transcending the typically slow process of natural selection. Given the inordinate rate of global change, environmental and social, caused by human activity, much of it involving extraordinary violence and dislocation, it is likely that mismatches between nature and non-nurturing environments are increasingly common. Environments to which human populations are reasonably well adapted biologically, and the lived environments in which millions of people are forced to exist owing to displacement in the interests of "development" or as the result of war, are not biologically tolerable. Data based on the Dutch Hunger Winter (discussed in chapter 3), the Great Chinese Famine, and other situations in which starvation is implicated provide historical evidence of this process.

Colonization and historical trauma

Colonization was frequently justified in earlier centuries as bringing civilization and religion to the "natives," even though its primary purpose in many geographical locations was the rapacious procurement of natural resources, with traumatic consequences for indigenous populations that have persisted for generations.

Canada is home to roughly 1.2 million individuals who identified with the category "Aboriginal" in the Canadian census of 2006. The majority live in communities that continue to contend with the devastating legacy of settler colonialism, including entrenched poverty and invidious discrimination that persists, although this has somewhat abated. This legacy is manifested in "mental health" problems of many kinds, including substance dependence, depression, violence, and extraordinarily high rates of suicide, especially among young people, estimated in some Inuit communities to be six times the rate in other parts of Canada. Independently, mental health professionals and First Nations communities have associated this pathology of epidemic proportions with the experiences of colonization that commenced five centuries ago.

Records kept by the Royal Canadian Mounted Police (RCMP) show that more than 1,180 women of aboriginal decent, the majority teenagers or in their twenties, many in foster care, have been killed or gone missing over the past thirty years. Recently, two more bodies were found, one a 15 year old pulled from a Winnipeg river, her remains wrapped in plastic, and the other, a 16 year old, with her skull in one place and her body in another, outside Kamloops, British Columbia. A third adolescent, then 15 years old, who had been left for dead after two brutal attacks in the same night, but who survived against all odds, spoke to the Assembly of First Nations in 2015, calling for a national inquiry into this horrific state of affairs; her courage is to be commended. The former Conservative government of Canada insisted that such an inquiry was not necessary, but the current Liberal government supports this move. Recent media reports make clear that among the apprehended perpetrators of these crimes to date, the majority have been white serial killers.

The concept of "historical trauma" calls attention to the cumulative and intergenerational psychosocial effects of past colonial subjugation that persist to the present day. Among the travesties was the introduction of infectious disease. Measles, to which indigenous peoples had never been exposed, was inadvertently transmitted, but the claim is made that smallpox was spread by blankets deliberately distributed to assist with the extermination of an unwanted "race." This history is contested, but undeniably the mortality rate from infectious disease was extraordinarily high. The Haida nation went from an estimated population of 20,000 prior to 1770 to less than 600 by the end of the nineteenth century.

This decimation was followed by extensive efforts to " 'whiten' the Indian," primarily by means of residential schools created expressly to "kill the Indian and save the child." Young children were rounded up by school administrators, RCMP agents, and agents of the despised Bureau of Indian Affairs to be sent great distances from their homes to be housed in institutions where they were not permitted to speak their own languages, or participate in "cultural practices." It came to light in a 2013 Truth and Reconciliation Commission of Canada that repeated sexual abuse took place in these schools, one of which was characterized by a Supreme Court Justice as practicing "institutionalized paedophilia." Systematic nutritional medical experimentation resulted in malnutrition and death for many students. TB was rampant, and few attempts were made to curb it. The majority who grew up in these conditions, now middle aged and older, have until recently been unwilling to reflect upon their younger lives, but many freely admit to being unable to adequately parent their own children. The residential schools, the last of which were closed in the 1990s, are regarded among First Nations and Inuit communities as the primary source of their current malaise. Despite major changes for the better in recent years, shocking poverty, racism, and discrimination continue to be blatantly evident on many reservations, the majority of which have no running water. Schools on reservations are poorly provided for compared to elsewhere in Canada, and the education gap has increased between First Nations children and other Canadians.

Not all reservations exhibit high rates of illness and suicide. Some survivors report that they enjoyed school, and among them many became devout Christians – a conversion that apparently assisted in their recovery.

Belatedly, in the 1960s, First Nations were given the right to vote; land claims settlements have improved the lot of some communities, and healing programs and suicide prevention gatherings conducted by First Nations themselves, which make use of both indigenous healing practices and biomedicine, exist in some communities and receive government support. Such changes are regarded positively by many, but are not yet broadly entrenched.

The then Prime Minister of Canada apologized to First Nations in 2008; nevertheless, the budgets of twelve government-funded programs have been cut and nine closed to date. If the concept of "historical trauma" is to be taken seriously, then a sustained effort to counter the effects of colonization being played out among third and fourth post-colonial generations is needed. It is not known if intergenerational transmission of epigenetic marks has occurred – understandably, involved families are reluctant to donate tissue for post-mortem analysis – but evidence of DNA methylation alone should not be diagnostic of the centuries-long effects of genocidal abuse. A deliberate, calculated desecration of nurture, of history, culture, language, families, and communities, inevitably wreaks havoc on the bodies of targeted people that undeniably has had intergenerational effects that First Nations today describe as "in the bone." Globally, similar effects of historical trauma are copious.

Biosocial becomings and situated biologies

For more than two decades, the anthropologist Tim Ingold has tussled with biological reductionism; he declared in 2013: "Neo-Darwinism is dead...brought down by the weight of its own contradictions"(2013: 1). In common with the majority of anthropologists, Ingold is particularly opposed to the reduction of the culture concept to a quasi-evolutionary process constituting a second form of inheritance. Reductionists argue that culture's components – "memes" – like genes, are *for* this or that, and hence they function to determine cultural evolution. The endless variety of life, including human life – endless forms most beautiful, as Darwin put it – is unaccounted for by the stultified memes of co-evolution. In opposition to such arguments, Ingold and one of the present authors (Ingold and Palsson 2013) adopt the concept "biosocial becomings" to convey the idea of an ensemble of commingled biological and social signatures. This metaphor better captures the relationship of the social and the biological, by associating environments beyond the body with molecular pathways steadily being exposed by epigeneticists.

Anthropologists have long carried out research in connection with the relationship among culture, self, and body, illustrating how discursive practices and symbolic systems serve to cement bodies in context. However, a biosocial body embraces broader dimensions of space and time, history and politics, and enlarges the very scale of what constitutes self and other by situating individuals as part of families, communities, and populations that have all too often been exposed to hugely disruptive events. This represents a major shift away from the standardized bodies of the biosciences. A closely related concept is that of "situated biologies," which goes beyond the stability of place that "local biologies" may suggest. "Situated biologies" implies that individuals in the contemporary world are subject to considerable change, forced or voluntary, over their lifetimes. The concepts of biosocial becomings, situated biologies, and embedded bodies encourage recognition of individuals, groups, and communities whose bodies are entangled in the past, present, and future. As we saw in the preamble, genomes exhibit evolutionary, environmental, historical, cultural, and political variables to which previous generations have been exposed over vast stretches of time. Bodies are receptacles, the basic form and structure of which is transmitted from generation to generation with relatively little change. However, epigenetic changes which take place during fetal development and over a lifetime as a result of environmental exposures are not transmitted intergenerationally, but frequently arise anew in successive generations, although experts disagree, and some argue strongly for the intergenerational transmission of certain epigenetic changes.

The question of persistence of similarities and difference has been at the heart of debate about heredity for centuries, as we have seen. As Richard Lewontin emphasized years ago, the environment cannot be independent of the organism, as the stark repercussions evident throughout the Anthropocene reveal, nor can the reverse be true. Moreover, epigenetic findings make clear that nature/nurture is commingled, and that we must go further and reverse this duo to become nurture/nature, thus acknowledging that nurture is the driving force for both individual development and for ceaseless transformations over generations.

FIVE

Biopolitics for the Future

An approach to the scientific investigation of the natural world was thoroughly consolidated by the late nineteenth century, at which time a dualistic opposition between nature and nurture became the dominant way of thinking, one that remains prevalent today. Although criticized by many, such thinking continues among numerous basic scientists who focus single-mindedly on the acquisition of molecular knowledge about the body largely in order to facilitate drug development and secondarily to refine disease diagnostics. In so doing, nurture, no doubt assumed by many of these scientists and their families as implicated in the conditions that afflict them personally, is set to one side.

Criticism by philosophers of science, social scientists, and certain life scientists of a nature/nurture opposition has accelerated over the past two decades, and accumulating empirical findings have contributed to a critique of this type of dualistic thinking.

Waddington's metaphor of the epigenetic landscape – his *geography* of life and thought – has proven staying power. A glance at Google shows hundreds of images of epigenetic landscapes. One depicts a pluripotent stem cell as the ball perched on a mountaintop. This image is associated with the award in 2012 of a Nobel Prize to John Gurdon and Shinya Yamanaka for their independent finding demonstrating that mature, specialized cells can be reprogrammed to become immature cells, capable of developing into any one of the tissues of the body: under controlled circumstances, the clock of epigenetically produced developmental differentiation can be turned back. These findings, which *reverse* the trajectory of Waddington's landscape, paradoxically confirm his original insights, making possible cloning and the reprogramming of cells for therapeutic purposes. Further evidence of a steadily escalating interest in epigenetics comes from the growing number of epigenetics journals, published papers, and conferences.

The previous chapters have shown how epigenetic research implicates political and social variables in embodied nurture/nature entanglements that reflect persistent health disparities, particularly evident in situations of environmental deprivation. It is well known that environments of poverty, discrimination, and violence result in poor health and early death, but epigenetics exposes the involved molecular pathways, confirming the indivisibility of nurture/nature. Such findings support demands for improved equity and justice that would also result in significant economic gains.

Whether or not molecularized epigenetics becomes mired in a form of neo-reductionism is open to question. Thus far the majority of behavioral epigeneticists select individuals or family units as the boundary of "nurture." Many acknowledge that broader political and economic factors impinge on families but cannot, as yet, isolate and measure the effects of these variables as molecular changes. Epidemiologists have, of course, created extensive statistical data about the impact of variables, including schooling, poverty, and discrimination, on selected populations, and a few of them are beginning to work with epigeneticists in teams, linking their findings. Philosophers of biology and social scientists cited in this book have focused on the ontology and epistemology of knowledge production in epigenetics, that is, on concepts and assumptions embedded in epigenetic research and goals, and the methods used to achieve these goals. The statement made by the neuroscientist Michael Meaney well over a decade ago spelling out what philosophers and social scientists have come to term the "reactive genome" has been cited many times: "At no point in life is the operation of the genome independent of the context in which it functions" (2001: 51). A few anthropologists are currently participating in research projects with epigeneticists, in which narrative accounts given by the people under study make a significant contribution to research findings, thus adding important information about the subjective experience of traumatic events, hence better situating biology in local contexts.

Molecular genetics and epigenetics will continue to bring scientific facts to light, but the hope must be for increased understanding of the value of different styles of reasoning and for communication across disciplines enabling molecular findings to be embedded in lived and narrated experience. Nature is understood as more flexible and malleable than has ever before been thought possible. Even so, in attempting to comprehend the new, at times aggressive, "nurture" that gets under the skin, scientists partition and measure it in order to bring about some semblance of order. Such an approach accounts for the effects of certain human behaviors on the wellbeing of the next generation, but it will not explain why the lives of so many people of that generation or the generation that went before them are in turmoil. This calls for a preventive approach that tackles the larger political and economic sources of distress, in addition to assisting individuals and families directly. Such efforts will not preclude drug development to reverse individual epigenetic changes, although much more knowledge is needed before such drugs could be handed out by clinicians to their patients.

Can science finally resolve the nature/nurture debate?

The last century has been described as the century of the gene. However, a 2015 editorial in *Nature* (518, 7539) argues that tackling diseases using information based on the genome alone is like "trying to work with one hand tied behind the back." The present century, if we survive it, may well be characterized by the damage that human-made environments cause to their own kind – the Anthropocene is a story of the rapacious nurture of powerful people playing havoc with nature. Nature in all its forms is exhibiting all the signs of stress, trauma, toxicity, and abuse that we usually associate with suffering human bodies; it is desperately signaling what is "unnatural."

At the molecular level, the nurture/nature debate currently revolves around reactive genomes and the environments, internal and external to the body, to which they ceaselessly respond. Body boundaries are permeable, and our genome and microbiome are constantly made and remade over our lifetimes. Certain of these changes can be transmitted from one generation to the next and may, at times, persist into succeeding generations. But these findings will not terminate the nurture/nature debate – ongoing research keeps arguments fueled and forces shifts in orientations to shift. Without doubt, molecular pathways will come to light that better account for the circumstances under which specific genes are expressed or inhibited, and data based on correlations will be replaced gradually by causal findings. Slowly, "links" between nurture and nature will collapse, leaving an indivisible entity. But such research, almost exclusively, will miniaturize the environment for the sake of accuracy – an unavoidable process if findings are to be scientifically replicable and reliable. Even so, increasing recognition of the frequency of stochastic, unpredictable events ensures that we can never achieve certainty.

The epigenetic process known as methylation is at work in the examples that appear in the previous chapters. Although there are other epigenetic mechanisms, including histone acetylation and deacetylation, that also regulate gene expression, they have not been researched to the same extent. At present, accumulating findings about chromatin are changing the field dramatically, and in closing we briefly consider this seismic shift now underway. In Charles Darwin's time, it was recognized that particulate hereditable matter, DNA as it is known today, is transformed over evolutionary time and hence is not stable. However, with the discovery of the double helix, and the assumption on the part of geneticists that DNA, "the source of life," is reproduced virtually unchanged throughout the life course, environmental effects were relegated to a secondary order, and conceptualized as layered over an invariant genetic foundation.

Emerging knowledge about chromatin challenges this assumption, which has already been weakened by molecular research. Chromatin, the "stuff" of chromosomes, the task of which is to compact DNA, is composed of DNA, RNA, proteins (among which are histones), and yet other molecules. Small amounts of DNA are wound around eight histones to form a bead-like structure known as the nucleosome, from which parts of the histone molecules protrude. Strings of nucleosomes are in turn twisted up to become chromatin fiber, compacted as a tight package (see Figure 2).

The study of chromatin has allowed scientists to investigate the way in which environmental exposures

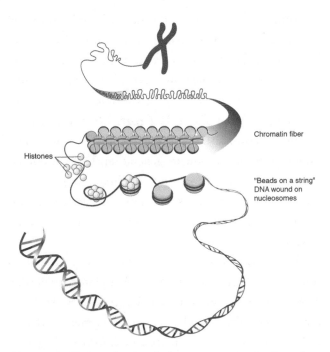

Figure 2. Various levels of chromatin organization, from chromosome to double helix
Source: Darryl Leja, NHGRI, genome.gov

originating outside the body bring about changes to the three-dimensional chromatin fiber (Lappé and Landecker 2015) that in turn influence the expression of DNA. Such exposures result in shifts in the spatial shape of DNA, proteins, and other molecules that determine whether or not genes will be transcribed and hence be active inside cells. Chromatin is no longer thought of as an inert scaffold, as was formerly the case, but is conceptualized as a dynamic body, profoundly influenced by environmental input, of which methylated DNA is a part. Moreover, certain features of chromatin – "epigenetic marks" – are transmitted from generation to generation. DNA methylation, found in all plants and vertebrates and in many non-vertebrates, is one such mark. Hence, chromatin carries experience forward over lifetimes and, at times, to future generations.

The genome can no longer be conceptualized as timeless – a fixed base upon which a plastic, malleable epigenome performs certain activities. Genes are "catalysts" rather than "codes" for development (Meloni 2014), and it is the structure of information rather than information itself that is transmitted (Lappé and Landecker 2015). Internally, strips of DNA can be altered, often during replication, some of which changes result in mutations that may or may not be hereditable. But DNA is not changed *directly* by environmental exposures. Rather, whole genomes respond ceaselessly to a wide range of environments, exposures, and experiences. Chromatin mediates such responses, which, in turn, influence DNA expression. The idea of an epigenome – a distinct layer over or enveloping the genome – as researchers, and increasingly the public, often think of it, is misconceived. The relationship of genome and epigenome is such that they are not independent of one another: this flexible, commingled entity, orchestrated by shape-shifting chromatin, has one and the same lifespan.

The implication of these insights is that teasing them apart for research purposes is inappropriate. Furthermore, to miniaturize the environment is problematic because experiences and events at a distance in time and space from individuals, families, and communities have profound, lasting effects, good and bad. As we noted in chapter 3, Georges Canguilhem emphasized that the "individuality of the living does not stop at its ectodermic borders any more than it begins at the cell." Canguilhem explicitly opposed biological reductionism when he argued that a milieu amounts to something greater than the sum of its parts. Today's milieu is a restless nurture/nature commingling of global proportions, one that never holds still in large part because of our ceaseless tinkering.

In this era of the Anthropocene, we are destroying local milieux beyond recognition, very often in the pecuniary interests of the few, while millions of individuals are left to survive in environments in which all semblance of a sustainable nature has been destroyed. We should listen carefully to nurture/nature debates as they unfold among the millions of displaced and dispossessed people in the world today and not simply monitor their bodies for signs of stress.

Science alone certainly cannot resolve nurture/nature debates; nor, for that matter, should such debates ever be resolved. They inform us how we are situated in the universe physically and morally. They will evolve based on scientific insights and hopefully on political and economic realities too, but we cannot do without them.

Ash, Lucy 2014. Why is Glasgow the UK's sickest city? BBC News, June 5. Online at http://www.bbc.co.uk/news/magazine-27309446.

Aviv, Rachel 2014. A valuable reputation. *New Yorker*, February 10.

Baedke, Jan 2013. The epigenetic landscape in the course of time: Conrad Hal Waddington's methodological impact on the life sciences. *Studies in the History and Philosophy of Biological and Medical Sciences* 44: 756–73.

Baltimore, David 2001. Our genome unveiled. *Nature* 409: 814–16.

Barnes, Barry and John Dupré 2008. *Genomes and What to Make of Them*. Chicago: University of Chicago Press.

Blackburn, Elizabeth H. and Elissa S. Epel 2012. Too toxic to ignore. *Nature* 490: 169–71.

Butler, Judith 1993. *Bodies That Matter: On the Discursive Limits of "Sex."* New York: Psychology Press.

Canguilhem, Georges 2008 [1965]. *Knowledge of Life*, trans. Stefanos Geroulanos and Daniela Ginsberg. New York: Fordham University Press.

Carey, Nessa 2012. *The Epigenetics Revolution: How Modern Biology Is Rewriting Our Understanding of Genetics, Disease and Inheritance*. London: Icon Books.

Cowan, Ruth Schwartz 1972a. Francis Galton's contribution to genetics. *Journal of the History of Biology* 5(2): 389–412.

Cowan, Ruth Schwartz 1972b. Francis Galton's statistical ideas: The influence of eugenics. *Isis* 63: 509–28.

159

References

Crick, Francis 1956. Central dogma of molecular biology. *Nature* 227: 561–3. Online at http://www.dna.caltech.edu/courses/cs191/paperscs191/CrickCentralDogma1970.pdf.

Crick, Francis and James Watson 1953. A structure for deoxyribose nucleic acid. *Nature* 171: 737–8. Online at http://www.nature.com/nature/dna50/watsoncrick.pdf.

Darwin, Charles 1859. *On the Origin of Species*. London: John Murray.

Davenport, Charles B. 1910. *Eugenics: The Science of Human Improvement by Better Breeding*. New York: Henry Holt.

de Beauvoir, Simone 1973 [1949]. *The Second Sex*, trans. H.M. Parshley. New York: Vintage Books.

Durkheim, Émile 1961 [1912]. *The Elementary Forms of the Religious Life*, trans. Joseph Ward Swain. New York: Collier Books.

East, E.M. 1917. Hidden feeblemindedness. *Journal of Heredity* 8: 215–17.

Forrester, Terence E., Asha V. Badaloo, Michael S. Boyne, et al. 2012. Prenatal factors contribute to the emergence of kwashiorkor or marasmus in severe undernutrition: Evidence for the predictive adaptation model. *Plos One* 7: e35907. doi10.1371.

Galton, Francis 1874. *English Men of Science: Their Nature and Nurture*. London: Macmillan

Galton, Francis 1876. A theory of heredity. *Journal of the Anthropological Institute of Great Britain and Northern Ireland* 5: 329–48.

Galton, Francis 1883. *Inquiries into Human Faculty and Its Development*. London: Macmillan.

Galton, Francis 1908. *Memories of My Life*. London: Methuen.

Gibbs, Wayt 2003. The unseen genome: Gems among the junk. *Scientific American*, November: 47–53.

Gilbert, Walter 1992. A vision of the grail. In Daniel J. Kevles and Leroy Hood, eds, *Scientific and Social Issues in the Human Genome Project*. Cambridge, MA: Harvard University Press.

References

Gilbert, Scott 2003. The reactive genome. In G.B. Müller and S.A. Newman, eds, *Origination of Organismal Form: Beyond the Gene in Developmental and Evolutionary Biology*. Cambridge, MA: MIT Press.

Gillette, Aaron 2007. *Eugenics and the Nature–Nurture Debate in the Twentieth Century*. New York: Palgrave Macmillan.

Gluckman, Peter and Mark Hanson 2008. *Mismatch: The Lifestyle Diseases Time Bomb*. Oxford: Oxford University Press.

Gould, Stephen Jay 1987. *An Urchin in the Storm: Essays about Books and Ideas*. New York: W.W. Norton.

Griffiths, Paul E. 2001 Developmental systems theory. In *Encyclopedia of Life Sciences*. London and New York: Nature Publishing Group.

Hall, Joseph 2013. The Human Genome Project: How it changed biology forever. *The Toronto Star*, 28 April. Online at http://www.thestar.com/news/insight/2013/04/28/the_human_genome_project_how_it_changed_biology_forever.html.

Harvey, William 1847 [1651]. Anatomical exercises on the generation of animals. In Robert Willis, ed, *The Works of William Harvey*. London: Sydenham Society.

Heijmans, Bastiaan T., Elmar W. Tobi, Aryeh D. Stein, et al. 2008. Persistent epigenetic differences associated with prenatal exposure to famine in humans. *Proceedings of the National Academy of Sciences* 105: 17406–9.

Hogben, Lancelot 1932. *Genetic Principles in Medicine and Social Science*. New York: Knopf.

Hughes, Vivian 2014. Epigenetics: The sins of the father. *Nature* 507: 22–4.

Ingold, Tim 2013. Prospect. In Tim Ingold and Gisli Palsson, eds, *Biosocial Becomings: Integrating Social and Biological Anthropology*. Cambridge: Cambridge University Press.

Ingold, Tim and Gisli Palsson, eds 2013. *Biosocial Becomings: Integrating Social and Biological Anthropology*. Cambridge: Cambridge University Press.

References

Jablonka, Eva and Marion J. Lamb 2014. *Evolution in Four Dimensions: Genetic, Epigenetic, Behavioral, and Symbolic Variation in the History of Life, Life and Mind.* Cambridge, MA: MIT Press.

Johansen, Bruce E. 2003. The Inuit's struggle with dioxins and other pollutants. *American Indian Quarterly* 26: 479–90.

Johnson, Scott C. 2014. The new theory that could explain crime and violence in America. *Matter*, February 18. Online at https://medium.com/matter/the-new-theory-that-could-explain-crime-and-violence-in-america-945462826399.

Keller, Evelyn Fox 1996. *Refiguring Life: Metaphors of Twentieth-Century Biology.* New York: Columbia University Press.

Keller, Evelyn Fox 2000. *The Century of the Gene.* Cambridge, MA: Harvard University Press.

Keller, Evelyn Fox 2002. *Making Sense of Life: Explaining Biological Development with Models, Metaphors, and Machines.* Cambridge, MA: Harvard University Press.

Keller, Evelyn Fox 2010. *The Mirage of Space between Nature and Nurture.* Durham, NC and London: Duke University Press.

Keller, Evelyn Fox 2014. From gene action to reactive genomes. *The Journal of Physiology* 592: 2423–9.

Kreiger, Nancy and Diane L. Rowley 1992. Re: "Race, family income, and low birth weight." *American Journal of Epidemiology* 136: 501–2.

Kroeber, Alfred 1917. The Superorganic. *American Anthropologist* 19: 163–213.

Kuhn, Thomas S. 1996. *The Structure of Scientific Revolutions.* 3rd edn. Chicago: University of Chicago Press.

Kuzawa, Christopher W. and Elizabeth Sweet 2009. Epigenetics and the embodiment of race: Developmental origins of US racial disparities in cardiovascular health. *American Journal of Human Biology* 21(1): 2–15.

References

Landecker, Hannah 2011. Food as exposure: Nutritional epigenetics and the new metabolism. *BioSocieties* 6: 167–94.

Lappé, Martine and Hannah Landecker 2015. How the genome got a lifespan. *New Genetics and Society* 34(2): 152–76.

Lewontin, Richard 1992. The dream of the human genome. *New York Review of Books*, May 28.

Lewontin, Richard 1995. Genes, environment, and organisms. In R.B. Silvers ed., *Hidden Histories of Science*. New York: New York Review Books.

Lewontin, Richard 2011. It's even less in your genes. *The New York Review of Books*, May 26.

Lock, Margaret 1980. *East Asian Medicine in Urban Japan: Varieties of Medical Experience*. Berkeley: University of California Press.

Lock, Margaret 1993. *Encounters with Aging: Mythologies of Menopause in Japan and North America*. Berkeley: University of California Press.

Lock, Margaret 2013. The epigenome and nature/nurture reunification: A challenge for anthropology. *Medical Anthropology* 32: 291–308.

Lutz, Pierre-Eric and Gustavo Turecki 2014. DNA methylation and childhood maltreatment: From animal models to human studies. *Neuroscience* 264: 142–56.

McGowan, Patrick O., Aya Sasaki, Ana C. D'Alessio, et al. 2009. Epigenetic regulation of the glucocorticoid receptor in human brain associates with childhood abuse. *Nature Neuroscience* 12: 342–8.

Mansfield, Becky 2012. Race and the new epigenetic biopolitics of environmental health. *BioSocieties* 7: 352–72.

Markowitz, Gerald and David Rosner 2014. *Lead Wars: The Politics of Science and the Fate of America's Children*. Berkeley: University of California Press.

163

References

Mauss, Marcel 1973 [1934]. Techniques of the body. *Economy and Society* 2: 70–80.

Meaney, Michael J. 2001. Nature, nurture, and the disunity of knowledge. *Annals of the New York Academy of Sciences* 935: 50–61.

Meaney, Michael J., Josie Diorio, Darlene D. Francis, et al. 1996. Early environmental regulation of forebrain glucocorticoid receptor gene expression: Implications for adrenocortical responses to stress. *Developmental Neuroscience* 18: 49–72.

Meloni, Maurizio 2014. How biology became social, and what it means for social theory. *The Sociological Review* 62(3): 593–614.

Mol, Annemarie 2002. *The Body Multiple: Ontology in Medical Practice*. Durham, NC and London: Duke University Press.

Monk, Catherine, Julie Spicer, and Frances A. Champagne 2012. Linking prenatal maternal adversity to developmental outcomes in infants: The role of epigenetic pathways. *Developmental Psychopathology* 24: 1361–76.

Morgan, Thomas Hunt 1910. Chromosomes and heredity. *The American Naturalist* 44: 449–96.

Muller, Hermann J. 1951 [1926]. The development of the gene theory. In Leslie C. Dunn, ed., *Genetics in the Twentieth Century*. New York: Macmillan.

Müller-Wille, Staffan and Hans-Jörg Rheinberger 2007. Heredity – The formation of an epistemic space. In Staffan Müller-Wille and Hans-Jörg Rheinberger, eds, *Heredity Produced: At the Crossroads of Biology, Politics, and Culture 1500–1870*. Cambridge, MA: MIT Press.

Müller-Wille, Staffan and Hans-Jörg Rheinberger 2012. *A Cultural History of Heredity*. Chicago: University of Chicago Press.

Niewöhner, Jörg 2011. Epigenetics: Embedded bodies and the molecularisation of biography and milieu. *BioSocieties* 6: 279–298.

Osborn, Fairfield 1948. *Our Plundered Planet*. London: Faber and Faber.

References

Palsson, Gisli 2016. *The Man Who Stole Himself: The Slave Odyssey of Hans Jonathan*. Chicago: University of Chicago Press.

Richardson, Sarah S. 2015. Maternal bodies in the postgenomic order: Gender and the explanatory landscape of epigenetics. In Sarah S. Richardson and Hallan Stevens, eds, *Postgenomics: Perspectives on Biology after the Genome*. Durham, NC and London: Duke University Press.

Rose, Steven, 1997. *Lifelines: Life beyond the Gene*. Oxford: Oxford University Press.

Sanger, Margaret 1922. *The Pivot of Civilization*. Washington, DC: Scott-Townsend Publishers.

Schrödinger, Erwin 2006 [1944]. *What Is Life?* Cambridge: Cambridge University Press.

Singh, Ilina 2012. Human development, nature and nurture: Working beyond the divide. *BioSocieties* 7: 308–21.

Spencer, Herbert 1864. *The Principles of Biology*, Vol. 1. London: Williams & Norgate.

Strohman, Richard 2001. A new paradigm for life: Beyond genetic determinism. *California Monthly* 111: 4–27.

Thomas, Julia Adeney 2014. History and biology in the Anthropocene: Problems of scale, problems of value. *American Historical Review* December: 1587–607.

United States Office of Technology Assessment 1988. *Mapping Our Genes*. Washington, DC: Government Printing Office.

Waddington, Conrad H. 1957. *The Strategy of the Genes: A Discussion of Some Aspects of Theoretical Biology*. London: George Allen and Unwin Ltd.

Williams, Raymond 1976. *Keywords*. London: Collins.

Wilson, E.O. 1978. *On Human Nature*. Cambridge, MA: Harvard University Press.

Wilson, P.K. 2007. Drink, dames and disease: Erasmus Darwin on inheritance. *Versalius* 13: 60–7.

Index

Index

Index

Index

Index

Index

Index

Index

Index

Index